CW00704308

# TEACH YOUR CHILD TO COOK

BY THE SAME AUTHOR

Fay Maschler's Guide to Eating Out in London
Cooking is a Game You Can Eat
Cooking is a Way Round the World
Howard and Maschler on Food (with Elizabeth Jane Howard)
Eating In

A PRIMER THAT WILL INSTRUCT AND INFORM AS

WELL AS AMUSE AND GENERATE REAL SATISFACTION

BLOOMSBURY

To my children,
Hannah, Alice and Ben
and to their friend and mine,
Hazel Short

First published in Great Britain 1988
Copyright © 1988 by Fay Maschler

Bloomsbury Publishing Ltd, 2 Soho Square,
London W1V 5DE

British Library Cataloguing in Publication Data
Maschler, Fay
Teach your child to cook.
1. Cookery — For Children
I. Title
641.5

ISBN 0-7475-0077-0

Designed by Roy Williams and Laurence Bradbury
Design assistant Sarah Collins
Illustrations by John Hannay

Typeset in Great Britain by Falcon Graphic Art Ltd,
Wallington, Surrey
Printed in Great Britain by Butler & Tanner Ltd,
Frome and London

# CONTENTS

# INTRODUCTION

I love cooking. I discovered it at the age of 12 when my parents took me from Britain to live in the USA and for a long summer I had to amuse myself, having not started at my new school or made any friends. With nothing much to do I decided to mess around in the kitchen. I began with quite complicated recipes from the dense and stuffy cookery books that my mother owned, but when items like meringues and puff pastry *worked*, did what was expected of them, I was encouraged and cooked on. When you are a child, much of what you do does not seem to attract adult approval. Cooking did — and this was a bonus on top of its being a 'game' that was interesting, creative, sometimes surprising and more often than not delicious. It felt good to hand round the results of my cooking afternoons: I felt I was the giver, while the adults were on the receiving end — the other way round from the usual situation.

I continued to cook off and on, and when I left home to share a flat with friends I was pleased to find that being able to make a meal was a real asset. A girl I was sharing with was also keen on cooking and so we were able to entertain friends regularly.

I married someone who liked to eat well! When my children were small I found that each one, boy as well as girls, would play for a long time at the pastime of cooking mainly because at the end of the measuring, weighing, mixing, shaping and cutting-out games there was something to eat, to save for later and to give to others. Later on, as they became older, they could make snacks and meals for themselves, which was satisfying both to them and to me. Also they were more inclined to be experimental about eating if they had had a hand in the preparation of the food.

Being able to cook is a gratifying and useful skill. It is almost like being able to speak another language — one that anyone else can understand. It is not difficult to learn — especially if, unlike me, you start with some basics and develop from there. Much in cookery can be broken down into 'building blocks'. For

example, once you know how to make a batter — a mixture of flour, egg and milk — you can make not only pancakes, sweet and savoury, but also Yorkshire Pudding, Toad-in-the-Hole, Popovers, Waffles, Fritters, Tempura and Panscones. When you have mastered a roux — the base for white sauce — you can make soups, soufflés and croquettes and combine the technique with the one outlined in Chapter Five and make Moussaka or Lasagne. With a few basic operations mastered, the possibilities are endless and your own imagination and daring become important ingredients.

Cooking should also be frivolous and explore the magical side of the chemistry of energy applied to ingredients. There are many examples in this book of amazing transformations — of egg-whites into a snow that enables you to bake ice-cream, as in a Baked Alaska, of sugar into golden threads that set hard, of syrup into honeycomb when bicarbonate of soda is stirred in. If you have never done it before, even making mayonnaise is startling. Who would have thought an egg-yolk could thicken oil into what is practically an ointment? Baking turns blobs of dough into crisp and lacy biscuits, and flour and water into bread, the staff of life.

Although there is so much pre-prepared convenience food available these days, it would be sad to miss out on the excitement of cooking and the rewards to be obtained from your own efforts. And even if you still resort to packaged food quite often, it is a comforting feeling to know that you can cook things — not just as well, but better — yourself.

The recipes and their illustrations aim to be as detailed as possible but here are a few tips to keep in mind:

Wash your hands before you begin cooking.

Read a recipe right the way through before you begin so that you are not caught short in the middle of doing it, discovering you lack a vital ingredient or piece of equipment.

Where the recipe indicates that it matters, remember to turn on the oven ahead of time so that it has reached the right temperature when you are ready to cook the ingredients.

Always have on hand sturdy oven gloves or a thick cloth for handling hot pans and anything that you put into or take out of the oven.

Sharp knives are actually safer than blunt ones, as less pressure is needed for cutting and chopping. However, remember that they *are* sharp and hold them carefully with the blade always pointing down. Cut on a soft surface such as wood or melamine. A hard surface such as stainless steel or marble will blunt the knives and also encourage them to slip.

In many of the recipes where butter is used it is interchangeable with vegetable oil and this is indicated. You may of course substitute margarine if you wish, although this will affect the flavour somewhat.

Use either the metric measurements or the imperial ones. Because it is impossible to convert the measurements with absolute precision, it is important not to mix the systems.

'Spoonfuls' means rounded spoonfuls unless otherwise indicated.

Be bold and experiment! Once you have learned the essentials and understood why certain ingredients behave as they do, the world is more than your oyster.

Learn from your mistakes. They will doubtless taste good anyway, so it is not a waste. Cooking from scratch is almost always cheaper than buying convenience foods, and since food is such a pleasure as well as a necessity it seems to me that it should be a priority in spending. One of the reasons British food is seen to be less exciting than, say, French or Italian, is that we spend less of our disposable income on eating in and eating out. Good food is important, both to health and to happiness.

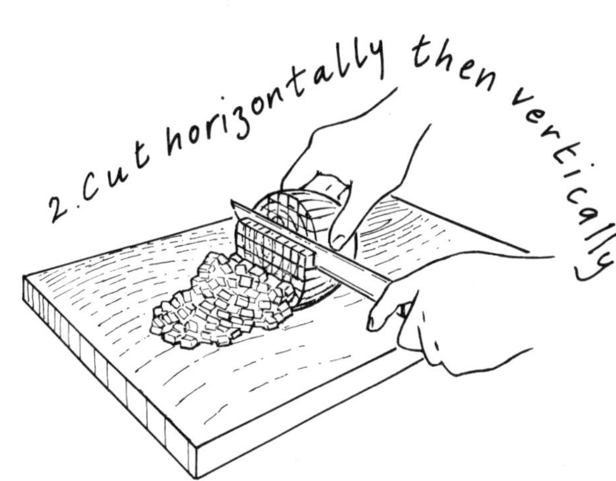


## Garlic

A 'clove' of garlic means one of the sections that make up the whole bulb — or 'head' — of garlic. If you crush garlic through a garlic press, trim each end of the clove but leave the papery skin intact. This makes the garlic-crusher easier to clean. If you need to peel the garlic clove, bash it gently with the back of a heavy kitchen knife. This will split the skin and enable you to take it off easily.

## Onion

There is a method of chopping an onion that gives neat small squares and minimizes the chance of tears being brought to your eyes. First, trim off the root end and the top of the onion and peel off the brown skin. Cut a small slice off one side to give you a level base on which to stand the onion. Now stand the onion on this flat side, with the root end pointing away from your chopping hand. Using a small sharp knife, cut the onion in slices horizontally towards the root, leaving the onion still attached at the root end. Now cut the onion vertically in slices from tip to root, but still leaving the onion intact at the root end. Next, cut the onion vertically in slices parallel to the root, but starting from the other end. The onion will fall into small squares. Finally chop the root end into small pieces.

Go to it!

CHAPTER ONE

# BATTER

BASIC BATTER · FRENCH PANCAKES

POPOVERS · YORKSHIRE PUDDING

TOAD-IN-THE-HOLE · FRUIT FRITTERS

TEMPURA · WAFFLES

CLAFOUTIS · PANSCONES

In the first three chapters — Batter, Roux and Dough — the basic ingredients used for the cooking are notably similar. Flour, eggs, fat, milk or other liquids appear and reappear, but when they are mixed in various ways the results can be quite startlingly different.

In the case of batter, the same mixture that cooks flat as a pancake will, when subjected to the heat of the oven, puff up into Yorkshire Pudding, Popovers or the crust around sausages that we call Toad-in-the-Hole. When batter is dropped into hot oil as for Fritters, the hot oil, which acts faster than oven heat, sets the batter in a different form which can be explained by the way in which air is trapped within the mixture. In Waffles and Panscones a raising agent, baking powder, creates the leavening through the formation of cells of gas which are sealed in by quick cooking or frying. Stiffly beaten egg-whites also contribute their Dunlopillo effect to the Fritters and Waffles.

The key to all these delicious effects, both savoury and sweet, is simply introducing the dry ingredient, flour, to the liquid ingredients, eggs and milk, in the correct, gradual manner. To do this when making batter by hand you have to 'draw in' the flour bit by bit. The egg is first of all put into a well made in the middle of the heap of flour, and the action of stirring it will begin to incorporate the flour that clings to the wet surface. When the egg becomes too thick with flour to be easily stirred you start to add milk. The final mixture should be smooth and have the consistency of thick cream. If you can work it into your planning, it is a good idea to make batter a couple of hours before you want to use it. Letting the mixture stand allows the flour particles to expand in the liquid and ensures a light, delicate result. However, satisfactory pancakes can also be made from recently mixed batter.

## BASIC BATTER

4 oz/110 g plain flour
1 egg (size 2)
½ pint/290 ml skimmed or semi-skimmed milk
1 tbsp vegetable oil
pinch of salt

Sift the flour into a medium-sized mixing bowl. Add the pinch of salt. Using a wooden spoon make a well in the centre of the flour. Break the egg and pour it into the well. Using the wooden spoon, start to beat the egg, slowly taking in the flour from around its edge. When some of the flour has been incorporated and the liquid part of the mixture has thickened, start adding the milk bit by bit. Keep stirring, taking in flour and adding milk when necessary to keep the mixture fairly fluid. When all the flour has been mixed in, beat the mixture vigorously to remove the lumps. Beat in the oil.

If the mixture is still lumpy, sieve it into another bowl or large jug. Let it rest, if time permits, before using.

### To Make Pancake Batter in a Liquidizer or Food Processor

Place all the ingredients in the goblet of the liquidizer or in the bowl of the food processor fitted with the metal or plastic blade. Blend only enough to mix the ingredients. Do not over-process or bubbles will spoil the texture of the pancakes.

1. Sift in flour
2. Add salt
3. Break egg
4. Beat in egg
5. slowly add milk
6. Stir in oil
OIL
Basic Batter

## FRENCH PANCAKES (CRÊPES)

Make the Basic Batter recipe and, if possible, let it stand for an hour or two before you make the pancakes. The point of using skimmed or semi-skimmed milk in the recipe is for reasons of health (less fat) and also to give the pancakes an extra lightness and laciness. If you have no skimmed milk, you can use half-and-half full-cream milk and water to make up the ½ pint/ 290 ml of liquid that you need.

To cook the pancakes, heat up a heavy-bottomed frying pan, preferably with a non-stick inner surface, about 6 or 7 in/15 cm in diameter. Wipe the pan with a little butter or oil (butter if you are eating them sweet, oil if savoury). You are not going to fry the pancakes, just prevent them sticking. When the pan is hot, take a small ladleful of batter (a generous tablespoonful) and pour on to the pan. Tilt the pan to spread the batter all over the surface and pour any excess back into the bowl. Cook for a minute or two until you see the pancake beginning to lift away from the pan at the edges. Using a spatula, lift the pancake to check that the underside is brown, turn it and cook the other side. This will colour in a different way — less evenly, more spottily. It is the surface cooked first that should be the public face of pancake! Use the first pancake to test the consistency of your batter (if too thick stir in a tablespoonful of water) and to 'season' the pan. The first pancake is usually not worth keeping. Use the rest of the batter as above, keeping the cooked pancakes warm in a clean tea-towel or by stacking them on a plate placed over simmering water or in a low oven. Pancakes can be successfully frozen, each one separated by a sheet of greaseproof paper.

### To Serve as a Dessert

Pancakes are good just with a squeeze of lemon juice and a dusting of sugar, or wrapped around jam or ice-cream or soft fruit or stewed fruit or a combination of these.

### To Serve as a Savoury Dish

Pancakes can be rolled around a meat filling such as the meat sauce in the recipe for Spaghetti Bolognese (p.60) or around Stir-Fried Vegetables (p.85) or the mixture of chicken or prawns in a white sauce used for the Vol-au-Vents recipe (p.25). Fill the pancakes, lay them in a row in an ovenproof dish. Dot with butter, scatter with grated cheese and heat through in a hot oven for 20 to 30 minutes.

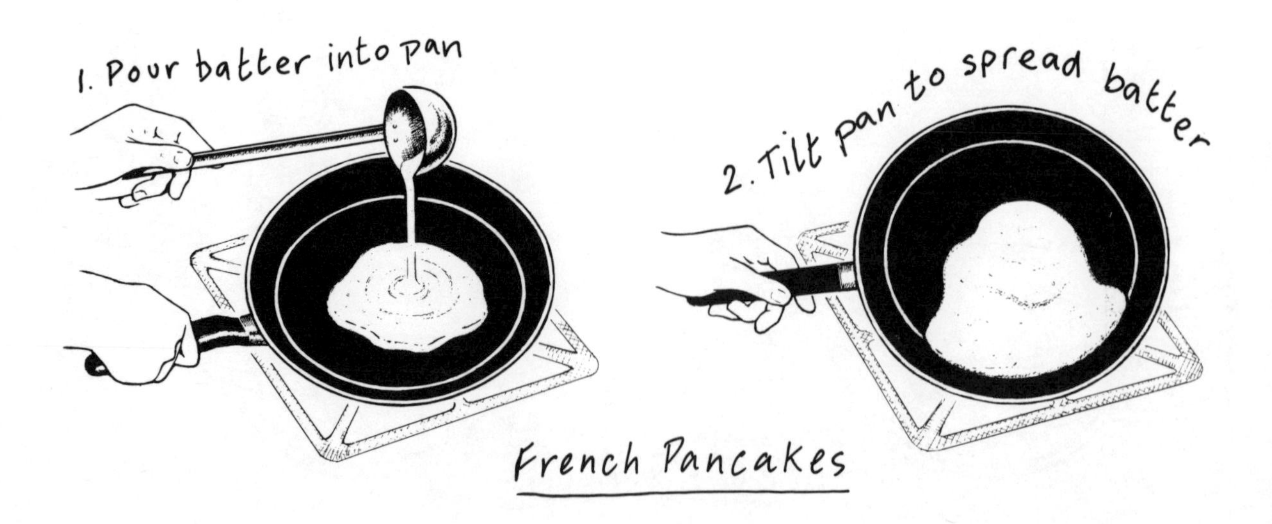

French Pancakes

## POPOVERS

You might think Popovers is just an American word for Yorkshire Pudding, but there are differences. Firstly, popovers are often eaten with butter for breakfast as well as being served as an accompaniment to roast beef. Secondly, they are made with butter in preference to other fats or oils. Thirdly, when you cook them you start them off in a cold oven which, oddly enough, gives the puffiest result and can come in handy if you are the sort of forgetful person who doesn't remember to pre-heat the oven!

Makes about 8 popovers

5 oz/140 g white flour
pinch of salt
2 eggs (size 2)
scant ½ pint/290 ml milk
1 tbsp melted butter

Sift the flour and salt into a large bowl. In another bowl whisk together the eggs, milk and melted butter. Add the liquid to the flour as you would for basic batter, making sure you do not overbeat as this does not help the popovers to pop. Use the mixture to half-fill the cups of a muffin pan or deep-cup baking tray. Put into a cold oven and set it at 450°F/230°C/gas mark 8. Bake for 15 minutes and then reduce the heat to 350°F/180°C/gas mark 4 and bake for another 15 to 20 minutes. Remove one popover to test that it is done. It should be crisp outside, moist within.

### For Cheese Popovers

Add 1 oz/30 g of grated cheese to the batter before cooking.

### For Wholewheat Popovers

Substitute wholemeal or wholewheat flour for two-thirds of the flour in the recipe, using white flour for the remaining third. Wholewheat popovers will not rise so dramatically but the loss of effect can be compensated for by the notion of virtue!

## YORKSHIRE PUDDING

Serves 4

Basic Batter recipe as above
3 oz/85 g beef dripping, lard or oil

Heat the oven to 400°F/200°C/gas mark 6.

Make the Basic Batter recipe and leave to stand for 30 minutes. In a small roasting tin or in individual Yorkshire pudding tins, heat the fat in the oven. When it is sizzling hot, pour in the batter and bake for 35 to 40 minutes (20 minutes if individual tins have been used) or until the batter is billowy and browned.

If you are roasting beef or any joint of meat in the oven, place the meat on the racks of an oven shelf and the tin of batter beneath, with a large pan on the floor of the oven to catch any spills. In this way juices from the meat will drip on to the batter, giving extra flavour and succulence.

## TOAD-IN-THE-HOLE

Basic Batter recipe as above, made up
6–8 sausages
2 tbsp vegetable oil

Turn on the oven to 475°F/240°C/gas mark 8.

Put the oil into a baking tin large enough to hold the sausages comfortably and place in the oven to get hot while the oven itself is heating up. Prick the sausages in a few places with a fork or the tip of a sharp knife. After 10 minutes, using a stout oven cloth or oven gloves, remove the tin from the oven. Place the sausages in the hot oil and return the tin to the oven for a further 5 minutes to pre-cook the sausages and ensure that they will be well done. Pour the batter all around the inside of the tin and return it to the oven immediately. Cook for 40 minutes, by which time the batter will have puffed up like clouds around the browned sausages.

## FRITTER BATTER

Serves 4–6

4½ oz/125 g plain flour
pinch of salt
2 eggs (size 2)
scant ½ pint/290 ml milk
1 tbsp vegetable oil
vegetable oil (about 1¾ pints/1 litre), for frying.

Sift the flour and salt into a bowl. Make a well in the flour, using a wooden spoon. Separate one of the eggs, putting the white into a clean medium-sized mixing bowl. Put the yolk and the other whole egg into the well in the flour. Start to stir the eggs with a wooden spoon and gradually draw the flour into the egg mixture (see Basic Batter recipe for more detail). Add the milk bit by bit once the egg and flour mixture is thick and continue drawing in the flour until the whole becomes a smooth, creamy batter. Add the oil. If there are any lumps still in the batter, sieve into another bowl. Allow to rest for half an hour or more. When you are ready to make the fritters, beat the egg-white until it stands in stiff peaks. Fold it gently into the batter using a metal spoon.

## FRUIT FRITTERS

Serves 4–6

Fritter Batter recipe, made up
¾–1 lb/340–450 g suitable fruit. This could be apples, bananas, pears, ripe apricots, fresh pineapple, plums
1 lemon or lime, for juice
granulated sugar, for sprinkling on the fritters
vegetable oil (about 1¾ pints/1 litre), for frying
cube of bread, for testing oil

Prepare your chosen fruit. For apples, peel, core and divide into eighths. For bananas, peel, cut into 2-in/5-cm chunks and halve the chunks lengthwise. Halve apricots and plums and remove the stones. Cut pineapple into rings about 1 in/2.5 cm thick, cut the rings into quarters, remove the skin and central core. Squeeze lemon or lime juice on to the fruit to stop it discolouring and to add flavour. Sprinkle on a little sugar. Heat up the oil in a deep fryer or large saucepan. When you think it is hot, test the heat by frying the cube of bread. If it turns golden in about 8 seconds and is surrounded by a wreath of bubbles, the oil is ready. Using tongs, dip each piece of fruit in the batter and fry a few pieces at a time, turning once, until crisp and golden. Drain on kitchen paper, sprinkle with a little more sugar for the crunch of it and serve.

## TEMPURA (JAPANESE FRITTERS)

Serves 4

Fritter Batter recipe, made up
¾–1 lb/340–450 g suitable vegetables. These might include onions, aubergines, carrots, green, red or yellow peppers, sprigs of parsley, broccoli, mange-tout peas, mushrooms
4 oz/110 g peeled prawns or fillets of white fish such as plaice, cod, halibut, haddock or sole (optional)
vegetable oil (about 1¾ pints/1 litre), for frying
cube of bread, for testing oil
soy sauce

Prepare your chosen vegetables for frying. Onions and aubergines should be cut into rings about ¼ in/0.5 cm thick. Green peppers must be de-seeded and trimmed of membranes and cut into strips or rings. Carrots should be peeled and sliced thinly lengthwise. Mushrooms should be wiped and cut in half. Broccoli should be cut into sprigs. Mange-tout peas can just be trimmed at each end. Lightly salt the vegetables.

If you are adding fish to the tempura, clean the prawns leaving just the tails on. Cut the fish into pieces about 3 in/7.5 cm long and 1½ in/ 3.5 cm wide. Lightly salt them.

Heat the oil and when you think it is hot, test with the cube of bread. It should brown lightly in about 8 seconds and be surrounded by a wreath of bubbles. Using tongs, dip the vegetables and/or fish into the batter piece by piece and fry them a few pieces at a time, turning once, until crisp and golden brown. Drain on kitchen paper. Keep the first batches warm while you fry the rest but then serve immediately with a saucer of soy sauce for dipping.

## WAFFLES

To make waffles you need a waffle iron. If you are serious about these pancakes, so delicious with maple syrup and grilled bacon or sausages at breakfast time, it is worth investing in an electric waffle-maker which guarantees almost foolproof results by virtue of its heat control. However, a hand-held waffle iron, a somewhat cheaper gadget, also works well. Buy the heaviest you can find. As with making the French pancakes (crêpes) the first try can usually be thrown away. Think of this as an investment in ascertaining the ideal temperature and timing.

Makes about 16 waffles

a generous 8 oz/225 g plain flour
2 tsp baking powder
½ tsp salt
2 tbsp caster sugar
3 eggs
14 fl oz/420 ml milk
6 tbsp melted butter

Sift the flour, baking powder, salt and sugar into a bowl. Separate the eggs, putting the yolks into one large bowl, the whites into another. Beat the egg-yolks with a whisk or hand beater. Add the milk and melted butter and whisk together. Using the spoon, gently stir in the flour mixture. Do not beat. Beat the egg-whites until they will stand up in snowy peaks. With a metal spoon fold them carefully into the batter. The mixture is now ready to be spooned into a pre-heated waffle iron or electric waffle-maker. A tablespoonful of batter will be the right amount of batter for most waffle irons as the mixture spreads when the iron is closed. Cook for 5 minutes. Remove from the waffle iron and repeat until the mixture is used up.

## CLAFOUTIS

Cherries are the usual ingredient in this French batter pudding but other fruits can be used. Soft fruits such as raspberries and currants are ideal. Stoned plums and apricots, if nice and ripe, would also work well.

Serves 4–6

2 eggs (size 2)
3 oz/85 g caster sugar
1½ oz/45 g plain flour
¼ pint/150 ml double cream
½ pint/290 ml milk
1 x 1 lb/450 g tin of stoned black cherries

Turn on the oven to 375°F/190°C/gas mark 5.

In a medium-sized mixing bowl, beat together the eggs and sugar using an electric beater or wire whisk. Add the flour and beat some more. Pour in the cream and mix that in well. Do the same with the milk. Give a final whisk. Drain the cherries from their liquid and place them in a shallow ovenproof dish. Pour the batter over and cook in the pre-heated oven for 35 minutes. The batter will rise and brown and the inside will be somewhere between custard and cake. Eat while hot or warm.

## PANSCONES

The mixture for these batter scones can be made in a moment. The scones, sometimes called drop scones, are delicious straight from the griddle or pan with butter and jam. Any left-over panscones can be fried for breakfast in either butter or bacon fat. Their slight sweetness goes well with the savoury elements of breakfast. Cream of tartar and bicarbonate of soda when used together have much the same action as baking powder and baking powder can be substituted although the result will be less perfect.

Makes about 20 scones

8 oz/225 g plain white flour
pinch of salt
1 level tsp bicarbonate of soda
1 level tsp cream of tartar
2 tbsp sugar
1 small egg
1 tbsp melted butter
½ pint/290 ml milk (skimmed or semi-skimmed if you prefer)

Beat the egg with the sugar and add in the melted butter. Mix the bicarbonate of soda with the milk and add this to the egg mixture. Sieve the flour, salt and cream of tartar into a bowl and add the egg mixture gradually, blending the ingredients together as for basic batter.

Let the batter stand for at least 10 minutes. Heat up a griddle or heavy-bottomed frying pan. Wipe it with a scrap of butter or a little oil on kitchen paper. Drop spoonfuls of the mixture on to the pan. You should be able to cook at least three scones at once. After a couple of minutes, when bubbles start to show on the tops of the scones and the undersides are golden, flip them over and brown the other side. You will need to oil or butter the pan again from time to time as you work your way through the batter.

CHAPTER TWO

# ROUX

BASIC WHITE SAUCE · BÉCHAMEL SAUCE

PARSLEY SAUCE · CHEESE SAUCE

MUSHROOM SOUP · VOL-AU-VENTS

CHEESE SOUFFLÉ · LASAGNE

CROQUETTES · GRATIN OF LEEKS

Roux is the mixture of butter and flour cooked together that forms the basis of a white sauce or béchamel sauce, the latter being a sauce in which herbs and flavourings have been added to the milk that is used as the liquid. A white sauce can be the starting point for various sauces such as parsley sauce, cheese sauce (also known as sauce Mornay), onion sauce (also known as sauce Soubise), anchovy sauce and egg sauce, but perhaps less obviously it is also both the foundation of some soups and a step on the way to a soufflé, and can be used as the topping for moussaka and lasagne or as the binding mixture for croquettes, gratins and the fillings in vol-au-vents.

A white sauce is easy to make and apart from turning out lumpy — which can be remedied — it can hardly fail to work.

That butter and flour cooked gently together will thicken a liquid is something in life upon which you can rely.

### Some Tips for a Good White Sauce

1. It is important to cook the flour with the butter for a few minutes before adding any liquid, as this both removes the raw and pasty taste that uncooked flour would give to a sauce or a dish and prepares the flour particles for absorbing the liquid.

2. The thickness of a white sauce depends on the amount of flour used in relation to the amount of liquid. For a pouring or coating sauce you need about 1 oz/30 g of flour to ½ pint/290 ml of liquid and for a soufflé base you increase the proportion of flour to 1½ oz/45 g per ½ pint/290 ml of liquid.

3. A sauce that is too thick can be diluted with added liquid. A sauce that is too thin can be reduced by simmering.

4. Use a heavy-based small to medium-sized pan to avoid scorching, as the lactose (milk sugar) in milk is liable to caramelize.

5. To save whisking time, the liquid can be added hot.

6. If lumps occur, do not cook them. Remove the pan from the heat and give a good whisk with a wire whisk or beat with a wooden spoon. If the lumps persist the sauce can be sieved.

## BASIC WHITE SAUCE

1 oz/30 g butter
1 tbsp plain white flour
½ pint/290 ml milk (skimmed or semi-skimmed if you prefer)
salt and pepper, for seasoning

In a small heavy-bottomed saucepan melt the butter. Stir in the flour and keep stirring over a low heat until you have a smooth mixture. Stir on for a few minutes to cook out any floury taste. Add a little of the milk and blend it in. Add some more and stir until you have a smooth but thick mixture. Add a little more and keep going until you have used up all the milk. Let the mixture come to the boil and then reduce the heat so that the sauce only just simmers. You should now have a smooth mixture of the consistency of double cream or, to put it another way, a mixture that will pour slowly from a ladle. Add a pinch of salt and pepper for flavouring.

1. Melt butter
2. Stir in flour
Low heat
3. Little milk
Then all the milk
4. Bring to boil
Then simmer
Basic White Sauce

## BÉCHAMEL SAUCE

1 oz/30 g butter
1 tbsp plain white flour
½ pint/290 ml milk
1 small onion, peeled
1 bay leaf
6 black peppercorns
salt and pepper
pinch of grated nutmeg

Measure the milk into a small heavy-bottomed pan. Add the onion, bay leaf and black peppercorns. Bring slowly to the boil and let it just simmer — no more than shuddering — for 5 to 10 minutes. Melt the butter in another sturdy pan. Stir in the flour and cook for a few minutes. Strain in the hot milk through a sieve and whisk it into the roux. Bring the sauce to the boil, still stirring, and flavour with salt, pepper and nutmeg. Simmer for another 3 to 5 minutes.

Note: If you want to make a béchamel sauce ahead of time, you can prevent a skin from forming on it by putting a small cube of butter on a fork and rubbing the butter over the surface of the sauce.

## VELOUTÉ

A velouté is a roux thickened with veal, chicken or fish stock rather than with milk. The process and the quantities are the same. The mushroom soup recipe is based on a velouté. In many of the savoury dishes, stock can replace some of the milk to good effect.

## PARSLEY SAUCE

Basic White Sauce or Béchamel Sauce as above
2 tbsp finely chopped fresh parsley
squeeze of lemon juice

When you have made the basic sauce (following the above instructions), stir in the chopped parsley and a squeeze of lemon juice. Simmer for a minute or two and serve. Lovely on boiled ham or bacon or with grilled fish or roast chicken.

Parsley Sauce

## CHEESE (MORNAY) SAUCE

Basic White Sauce or Béchamel Sauce as above
1 oz/30 g grated hard cheese (e.g. Cheddar, Gruyère, Parmesan), or more for a stronger flavour
1 level tsp Dijon mustard (optional)

When you have made the basic sauce, remove from the heat and stir in the cheese and mustard. Keep stirring until the cheese has melted. Taste for seasoning.

Mornay sauce is good on vegetables (think of cauliflower cheese), white fish, chicken and hard-boiled or poached eggs.

## MUSHROOM SOUP

Serves 4–6

2 oz/55 g butter
12 oz/340 g mushrooms
1 clove of garlic, peeled and crushed
2 level tbsp flour, brown or white
1¾ pints/1 litre chicken stock (use a good make of stock cube if necessary)
salt and pepper
pinch of grated nutmeg
¼ pint/150 ml cream
1 tbsp finely chopped parsley

Wipe the mushrooms clean and chop them finely. Melt the butter in a medium to large saucepan and add the garlic. Stir around until it is softened and then add the mushrooms. Cook the mushrooms, stirring, until they are softened. Pour in the flour and blend it into the mushroom mixture. Heat the stock in a separate pan and then slowly pour it on to the mushrooms, stirring all the while. Let the mixture simmer for about 10 minutes. Add the cream and reheat. Season with salt and pepper and nutmeg. Sprinkle on the chopped parsley just before serving.

Note: Using a roux as a soup base works with various vegetables such as courgettes, cauliflower, broccoli — in fact any vegetables that are not in themselves starchy such as potatoes or parsnips. Left-over cooked chicken treated this way makes a good cream-of-chicken soup. These are not *great* soups, but are a world away from tinned varieties.

## VOL-AU-VENTS

Vol-au-vent cases, which you can buy ready-made frozen, are a useful item to keep in the freezer. They make a crisp and loving container for prawns, chicken or other savoury items or left-overs mixed into a white sauce or béchamel.

1 packet frozen vol-au-vent cases
Basic White Sauce as above
4–6 oz/110–170 g cooked chicken chopped
4 oz/110 g frozen prawns, defrosted *or* 6 oz/170 g fresh prawns, peeled

*Optional additions*
1 small tin of sweetcorn, drained *or* 1 small packet frozen peas *or* 4 oz/110 g button mushrooms, chopped and fried gently in butter

Heat the oven to the temperature indicated on the vol-au-vent packet.

Following the cooking instructions (the pastry can be cooked from frozen) prepare the vol-au-vent cases. While they are in the oven, divide the prepared sauce between two small saucepans and bring the sauce in both pans to simmering point. Add the chicken to one pan, the prawns to the other, together with any of the optional additions you have chosen, and gently heat through. When the pastry cases are cooked, remove them from the oven, arrange on a serving plate and fill with the chicken and prawn mixtures.

## CHEESE SOUFFLÉ

You should not be nervous of soufflés. Because they look so sensational, cooks through the ages have stressed their flightiness, their unpredictability and, consequently, when successful, the cook's skill. However, if the oven is at the correct temperature and in folding in the egg-whites you do not flatten them, it is unlikely that your soufflé will be a flop. One important thing to remember is that time, tide and soufflés wait for no man. Have your friends ready for the soufflé rather than expect the soufflé to wait around for your friends.

Serves 4

1½ oz/45 g butter
1 oz/30 g plain white flour
½ pint/290 ml milk (skimmed or semi-skimmed if you prefer)
3 oz/85 g hard cheese, grated (Cheddar, Gruyère, Parmesan or a mixture)
4 eggs (size 2 or 3)
pinch of salt
pinch of cayenne pepper or ordinary black pepper
scrap of butter, for greasing the dish
a little extra grated cheese, for coating the inside of the dish

Turn on the oven to 425°F/220°C/gas mark 7.

Using kitchen paper smeared with a scrap of butter or a bit of the paper that the butter is wrapped in, grease the inside of a straight-sided soufflé dish about 6 in/15 cm in diameter. Spoon in a little grated cheese and shake it around so that it sticks to the buttery surface. This will give the soufflé a nice crust.

Make a roux with the butter and flour, and add milk following the instructions in the Basic White Sauce recipe. Add the cheese and stir until it melts. Taste and see if the mixture could use some salt, remembering that the egg-whites will blur the flavour, and if so, add a pinch of salt and a pinch of cayenne or ordinary pepper. Remove the pan from the heat.

Separate the eggs, putting the four whites into a large clean bowl and the yolks into another, smaller bowl. Beat three of the egg-yolks, one by one, into the cheese mixture. Save the fourth egg-yolk in a cup covered with clingfilm. (You could use it for mayonnaise, add it to scrambled eggs, or glaze pastry or dough with it.) With a rotary beater or electric hand whisk, beat the egg-whites until they stand in snowy peaks. Take two tablespoonfuls of the egg-whites and carefully fold them into the cheesy mixture. This will lighten it and enable you to fold in the rest of the egg-whites more easily and without squashing the 'bounce' out of them. Pour the soufflé mixture into the prepared dish. Put it in the oven and turn down the heat to 400°F/200°C/gas mark 6. Bake for 25 minutes, resisting opening the oven door to have a look. When the soufflé is ready it will be golden brown, puffed up and just a little sloppy inside.

## MOUSSAKA

It is aubergines as an ingredient and the soft golden creamy topping that are the distinguishing marks of moussaka in the meat-pie stakes. Here, the inclusion of beaten eggs gives a lift, quite literally, to the white sauce.

Serves 4

**Base**
see recipe in Chapter Five (p.63)

**Topping**
Basic White Sauce as above
2 eggs (size 2 or 3)
1 oz/30 g grated Parmesan or other hard cheese

Make a white sauce according to the basic recipe. Crack the eggs into a mixing bowl and beat well with a whisk until foamy. Take the sauce off the heat and stir in the beaten eggs with a wooden spoon. Pour the topping on to the moussaka mixture, sprinkle with cheese and bake for 35 mintues at 350°F/180°C/gas mark 4. The topping will puff up a little owing to the inclusion of the beaten eggs and turn a golden brown.

## LASAGNE

Lasagne is less of a pasta dish than a pie, in which you use sheets of pasta dough to interleave the layers of meat sauce and white sauce. It makes a substantial meal and can successfully be made ahead of time and heated up. You can either use the pasta recipe in Chapter Three, and cut out rectangular sheets of fresh pasta dough for the lasagne, or buy the dried variety — either white or green (spinach flavoured). Simmer the Bolognese sauce for longer than usual when using it for lasagne, to make a drier mixture.

Serves 4

Bolognese sauce (see recipe in Chapter Five)
Basic White Sauce as above
8 oz/225 g lasagne dough
pinch of salt
scrap of butter
1 oz/30 g grated Parmesan cheese

Turn on the oven to 375°F/190°C/gas mark 5.

Using the scrap of butter, grease the inside of a rectangular ovenproof dish measuring about 9 in x 12 in/23 cm x 30 cm. Bring a large pan of water to the boil and add a generous pinch of salt. Drop in three or four sheets of lasagne. Cook until tender — 3 minutes for home-made pasta, 10 minutes or longer for packet pasta. Fish them out and drain on kitchen paper or a clean tea-towel. Repeat until all the pasta is cooked. Put a layer of pasta in the bottom of the dish. Spread with a thin layer of meat sauce. Cover this with a layer of white sauce. Lay on another layer of pasta and continue in the same way, finishing with a layer of sauce. Sprinkle on the Parmesan cheese and bake for 20 to 25 minutes until the filling is bubbling and the white sauce topping is golden. Serve hot or warm.

## CROQUETTES

Croquettes use a thicker version of white sauce for binding the main ingredient or ingredients, which are then wrapped in an egg-and-breadcrumb coating and fried. They are crunchy and light and can be an ideal way of using left-overs — in place of haddock you might use a mixture of hard-boiled egg and diced ham, prawns, cooked chicken or cooked spinach — but they are so good that they are worth making deliberately and from scratch.

Makes about 12 croquettes

### Filling

Basic White Sauce as above, substituting the milk the fish is cooked in for the milk in the recipe
6 oz/170 g smoked haddock
2 tbsp finely chopped parsley

### Coating

flour
salt and pepper
1 egg
dry breadcrumbs
vegetable oil, for frying

Put the smoked haddock in a wide, shallow pan and cover with the ½ pint/290 ml of milk from the Basic White Sauce recipe. Bring the milk just to a simmer, cook for a minute or two and then turn off the heat and cover the pan with a plate. Let it stand for 10 minutes, by which time the fish will be tender. Remove the fish from the milk and break into flakes. Make up the roux as described above and use the fishy milk for the added liquid, just enough to make a thicker sauce than usual as this is a binding mixture, not a pouring or coating one.

Mix the fish and parsley into the sauce. Spread the mixture into a shallow dish and chill either in the refrigerator for several hours or in the freezer for about 30 minutes.

When you are ready to cook the croquettes, find three shallow soup plates. Put three tablespoonfuls of flour in one, and season the flour with salt and pepper. Into another, break an egg and whisk it with a fork until well beaten. In the third, cover the base of the plate with dry breadcrumbs. Take the croquette mixture from the refrigerator. Shape the mixture into small patties. Dip each one first into the flour on both sides, then into the egg, then into the breadcrumbs. Heat up some oil — about 1½ in/4 cm deep — in a large pan. Fry the croquettes two or three at a time, turning once, until golden on the outside and heated through. They will take about 4 minutes each in total. Drain on kitchen paper and serve when all are ready. They are good with a spicy tomato sauce — see Chapter Seven (p.000).

## GRATIN OF LEEKS

This recipe can be used for various vegetables. Cauliflower, courgettes, spinach, broccoli and carrots are all delicious prepared this way. Cook the vegetables until just tender and make sure they are well drained before mixing them into the white sauce or béchamel sauce.

Serves 3–4

1 lb/450 g leeks
Basic White Sauce or Béchamel Sauce as above
2 oz/55 g grated hard cheese (e.g. Cheddar, Gruyère, Parmesan)
1 oz/30 g butter

Turn on the oven to 425°F/220°C/gas mark 7.

Clean the leeks, first cutting off the root end and trimming the stalk end about 1 in/2.5 cm from where it starts to be dark green. Make a lengthwise cut through each leek starting about half-way up the leek from the root end. This will help in the cleaning. Plunge the leeks into cold water and fan out the top ends to get rid of any lurking grit. Cook the clean leeks in plenty of boiling water for about 10 minutes or until tender. Drain thoroughly.

Into a shallow ovenproof dish, spoon a little of the white sauce and spread it around. Cut the leeks into 1-in/2.5-cm lengths and scatter them on top. Coat with the rest of the sauce. Sprinkle with cheese and dot with the butter cut into little pieces. Bake in the pre-heated oven for 10 to 15 minutes or until the gratin is golden on top and bubbling.

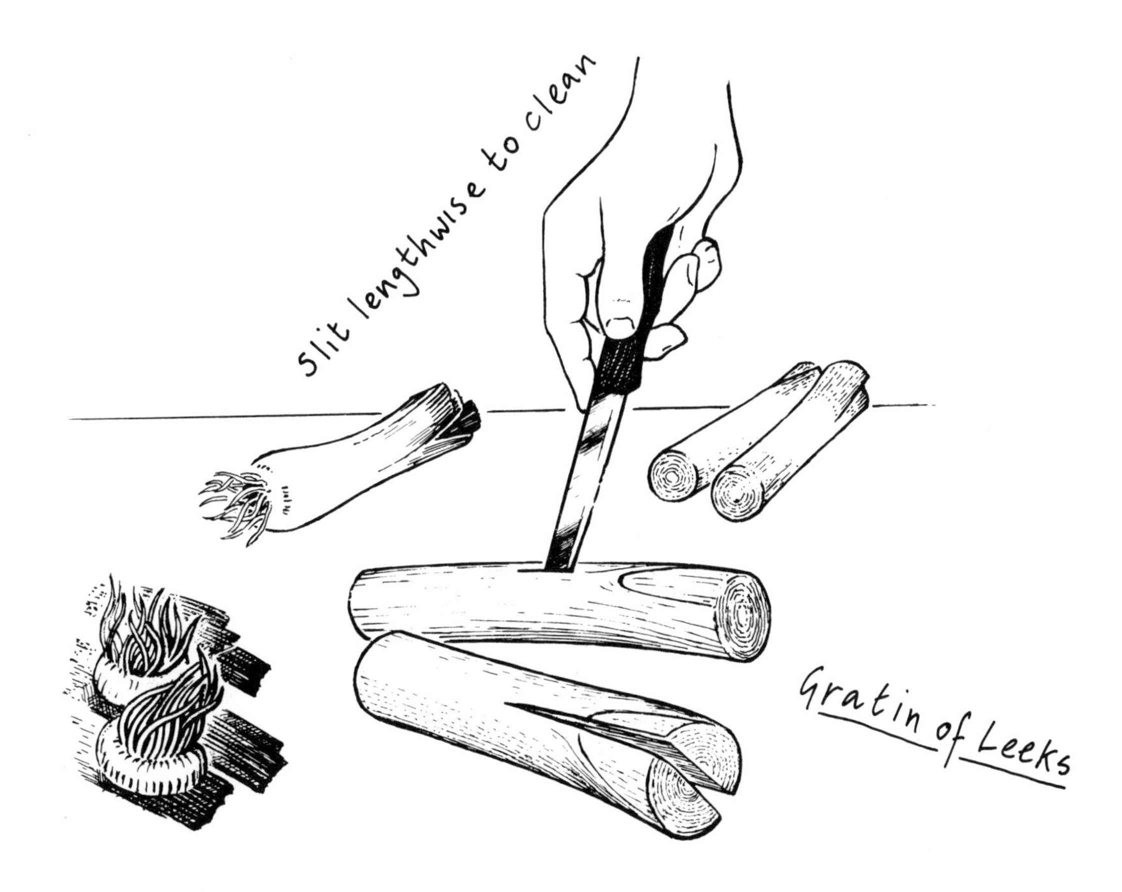

CHAPTER THREE

# DOUGH AND PASTA

---

BASIC BREAD DOUGH · DUMPLINGS

SODA BREAD · CHELSEA BUNS

CORNBREAD · CHAPATIS

PURIS · SHORTCRUST PASTRY

PASTA

Mixing mud and water makes mud pies. Mixing flour and water can make dough. The one activity can lead effortlessly into the other and making dough, for very many reasons, is the more gratifying activity. Transforming a fairly unpromising-looking heap of flour into the staff of life, the daily bread, is one of the more dramatic aspects of cooking and a therapeutic one too. If this old world is getting you down then there is nothing better than kneading dough, knocking it down, slapping and shaping it and then later removing from the oven a crusty loaf with a smell that speaks of wholesomeness.

Flour and water alone can make a dough that rises when heated (see recipes for Chapatis and Puris on p.000) but usually dough has a leavening agent. This can be bicarbonate of soda, which acts instantaneously so that you can bake a batch of soda bread within the hour, or yeast, which takes its time to perform. The particular kind of fungus that is yeast has a gas-producing metabolism that studs the dough with the air pockets that cause it to rise. Yeast sleeps in the cold, acts when warm and is killed by high heat. Fresh yeast is therefore stored in the refrigerator but the more widely available dried yeast can be kept for long periods in the store cupboard and reconstituted when needed.

When you soak dried yeast — usually letting it 'feed' on a little sweetness — it will froth up looking something like the head on a glass of beer, which has itself been used since Egyptian times to leaven bread. Depending on the warmth of the atmosphere, dough will rise more slowly or more energetically, and thus a yeast dough need not be a dictator; it can be obliged to fit in with your timetable.

Making bread is often avoided on the grounds that it is a lengthy process, but the amount of time you spend actually working is small, and by master-minding the temperature you can choose when you want to be occupied. For example, you can store prepared dough overnight in the refrigerator before letting it rise the next day.

Dough is also very amenable to variations in flour and flavour. Once you have got the hang of kneading dough, you might want to try out different flours such as wholemeal, rye flour and maize flour, different additions such as nuts, dried fruit, grated carrot, herbs, grated cheese and chopped fried onion and various seeds for toppings such as sesame, poppy and mustard. The number of possibilities is infinite and the pleasure in handing round freshly baked home-made bread cannot be underestimated.

## BASIC WHITE FLOUR BREAD DOUGH

Making a small amount of dough underlines the ease of baking, and the amounts below even very small hands can handle. If you like, substitute wholemeal flour for two-thirds of the white flour. Seeds such as sesame seeds scattered on to the glaze make the crust very tasty.

8 oz/225 g strong white flour
½ pint/290 ml tepid milk and water, mixed
pinch of white or brown sugar
1 heaped tsp dried yeast
1 tbsp sunflower oil
½ tsp salt
1 egg, beaten or 1 tbsp milk, for glazing

Turn on the oven to 350°F/175°C/gas mark 4.

continued over...

Basic White Flour Bread Dough (continued)

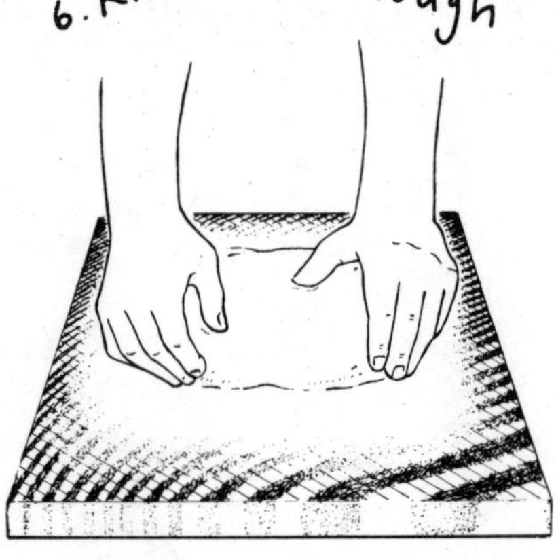


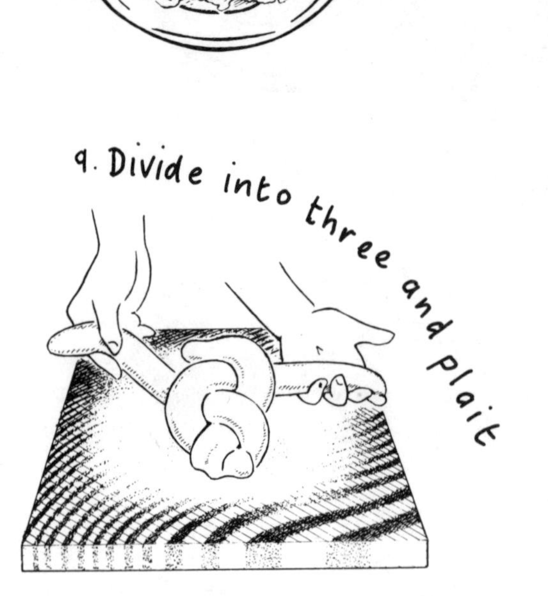


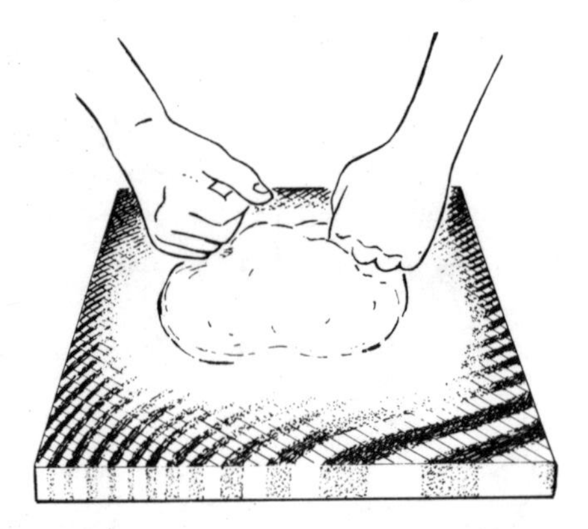

Put the milk and water mixture and the sugar into a small mixing bowl. Sprinkle on the dried yeast and let it dissolve in the liquid for about 10 minutes. A froth will form on the surface, rather like the head on a glass of beer. Sift the flour and salt into a larger bowl and pour on the yeasty liquid. Add the oil. Stir first of all with a knife, and then, when it looks as though you can handle the mixture, use your fingers to mix it all together.

When the dough has formed one lump, take it out of the bowl and start to knead it on the work surface. Keep pushing it with the heel of your hand and bringing it back into a ball until the dough is smooth and elastic and the surface shiny. Place it in a lightly oiled bowl, cover that with clingfilm or a clean tea-towel and leave in a warm place for an hour.

After that time, when the dough will have doubled in size, 'knock it down' by punching it with your fist and giving it another quick kneading. It is now ready to be shaped into a small loaf, some buns or a plait. For a plait, divide the dough into three and plait it loosely, pinching the ends together and tucking them under. Brush the top of the loaf with beaten egg or milk and place on a baking sheet. Let it sit in a warm place for about 40 minutes. Bake for 20 minutes. Take it out and turn it over, tap the bottom of the loaf and if it sounds hollow, it is done. If not, place it back in the oven, bottom side up, for another 5 to 10 minutes.

## DUMPLINGS

Make as many as you need

piece of dough from the Basic Bread Dough recipe
1 tbsp chopped fresh parsley

Mix the parsley into the dough. Pinch off pieces and roll them into balls the size of a large marble. Cook them either in simmering water or in a simmering stew or soup for 20 minutes with the lid on the pan. The dumplings should swell dramatically, but you must keep the lid on the pan until the moment of serving.

## SODA BREAD

Soda bread, as the name implies, uses bicarbonate of soda — the main ingredient in baking powder — and baking powder as the raising agents. What in effect is happening is the creation of self-raising flour, and soda bread needs no waiting for it to rise. The texture and flavour are somewhat different from those of yeast-raised bread — rather more chewy and salty — and the keeping qualities are not as good — but keeping soda bread is not usually an issue. This bread is very popular in Ireland.

10 oz/290 g wholemeal flour
6 oz/170 g plain white bread flour
3 tsp baking powder
1 tsp bicarbonate of soda
2 tsp salt
1 pint/570 ml buttermilk or milk soured with lemon juice
1 egg, beaten

Turn on the oven to 375°F/190°C/gas mark 5.

Sift together the two flours, baking bowder, bicarbonate of soda and salt. (If you are using a coarse brown flour don't bother with the sifting.) Mix together the buttermilk or soured milk and the egg and stir them into the dry ingredients. Mix roughly with a knife and then push together with your hands and knead on a floured surface for a few minutes until you have a fairly smooth ball. Shape it into a round, flattish cake and put on to a greased or non-stick baking sheet. Using a knife, make a deep cross on the top of the bread. Bake for 35 to 40 minutes.

## CHELSEA BUNS

Makes 8

Basic Bread Dough as above, left to rise for an hour
1½ oz/45 g butter
1½ oz/45 g caster sugar
½ tsp ground mixed spice or ground cinnamon
2 oz/55 g sultanas and 2 oz/55 g currants *or* 4 oz/110 g mixed dried fruit

Turn on the oven to 425°F/220°C/gas mark 7.

Grease a baking sheet with a little butter. Punch down the risen dough and roll it into a square. Mix together the butter and sugar and dot the mixture over the surface of the dough. Scatter the dried fruit and the cinnamon or mixed spice over the dough. Roll up the dough like a Swiss roll and cut it into slices about 1½ in/3.5 cm thick. Arrange the slices cut side up on the baking sheet and leave to 'prove', i.e. to rise a little, for 15 minutes. Sprinkle with caster sugar. Bake in the pre-heated oven for 20 to 25 minutes. Cool the buns on a wire rack and separate when cool.

## CORNBREAD

This is another quick bread to make using baking powder as the muscle. Americans are very fond of eating slightly sweet breads with savoury dishes and it is a habit easy to adopt. Corn meal is usually sold in health-food stores. Polenta is the Italian name for corn meal and you may find the grain sold under this name in supermarkets and delicatessens. Serve this caky bread hot from the oven with butter to melt on to it. A great treat.

2½ oz/75 g plain flour
7 oz/200 g corn meal or polenta
1 tsp salt
1 tsp sugar
2 tsp baking powder
2 eggs (size 2)
8 fl oz/250 ml milk
2 fl oz/60 ml cream
2½ tbsp melted butter
scrap of butter, for greasing the tin

Turn on the oven to 400°F/200°C/gas mark 6.

Using a scrap of butter on some kitchen paper, grease a baking tin 8½ in x 11 in/21.5 cm x 28 cm. Sift the flour, corn meal or polenta, salt, sugar and baking powder into a mixing bowl. Beat the eggs in another bowl and add the milk to them. Stir the eggs and milk into the flour with a wooden spoon. Beat in the cream and then beat in the melted butter. Pour the mixture into the prepared tin and bake for 15 to 20 minutes. Remove from the oven, cut into squares while still hot and serve the cornbread wrapped in a cloth napkin.

## CHAPATIS AND PURIS

Chapatis and puris are just two examples of the many kinds of unleavened bread that exist. Jewish matzo bread and Mexican tortillas are two others that might come to mind. Considering the simplicity of the ingredients the results are particularly impressive, and in the case of puris their ability to puff up in hot oil can be spectacular. It is important to have the patience to knead the bread thoroughly. Letting it rest before rolling and cooking does no harm, but always store it in a plastic food-bag to prevent it from drying out. Chapatis and puris make a good accompaniment to any spicy food.

### CHAPATIS
Makes 12

10 oz/290 g wholemeal flour
½ tsp salt
about 6 fl oz/175 ml hot water
2 tbsp melted ghee (clarified butter), butter, margarine or oil

Sieve the flour and salt into a bowl. Add most of the hot water and stir with a knife to blend. Using your fingers, pinch the dough together and add the rest of the water if the dough seems dry and crumbly. Take the dough out of the bowl and knead on a flat surface for about 10 minutes until the ball of dough is smooth and not at all tacky. Divide the dough in half and then each half into six so that you have 12 balls. With a rolling-pin roll them on a floured board into circles about 6 in/15 cm in diameter. Pat them between your palms to flatten them even more.

Heat a thick-bottomed frying pan over a medium heat. Take one chapati and fry it in the dry pan for about two minutes. Brown spots will appear on the underside. Turn it and cook the other side for the same amount of time.

Place the chapati on a plate and brush with a little melted ghee, butter, margarine or hot oil. Repeat with the rest of the chapatis.

### To Puff Up the Chapatis

Heat the grill until very hot. When you have fried a chapati, place it under the pre-heated grill for a few seconds. It will puff up. Turn and repeat on the other side. Brush with melted fat or oil as above.

## PURIS

The same dough as above, when fried in hot oil as described below, will puff up and make puris, but you can also add oil to the dough for extra richness:

Makes 16

8 oz/225 g wholemeal flour
½ tsp salt
2 tbsp vegetable oil
about 3½ fl oz/90 ml hot water
vegetable oil, for deep frying

Sieve the flour and salt into a mixing bowl. Stir in the oil with a knife. Add most of the water and mix with your hands to make a fairly stiff dough, adding more water if the dough seems too dry. Knead for 10 minutes on a hard surface until the dough is smooth and flexible. Divide the dough in half and then each half in half again and so on until you have 16 small balls. On a lightly oiled surface roll each ball into a round about 4 in/10 cm in diameter. Keep the rounds separate or you risk their sticking together.

Pour the oil into a medium-sized frying pan, to a depth of 1 in/2.5 cm, and heat it. When it is very hot, slide in one puri. Press it down with a slotted spoon. It will puff up dramatically. Turn the puri and cook it for another 15 seconds. Drain on kitchen paper and serve while hot and airy.

## SHORTCRUST PASTRY

The process of making pastry is akin to that of making dough, but requires the technique of rubbing fat into flour and benefits from less handling — it doesn't need kneading. The pastry recipe below is a straightforward one, ideal for tarts, tartlets, pies and quiches. If you are making a sweet tart you could add two teaspoonfuls of icing sugar to the flour and use an egg-yolk together with whatever is necessary in iced water for the liquid.

8 oz/225 g plain flour
pinch of salt
2 oz/55 g butter and 2 oz/55 g lard
splash of iced water

### By Hand

Sift the flour and salt into a bowl. Cut the butter and lard into cubes and add to the flour. Using a knife, cut them about in the flour until they are covered in flour and roughly mixed. Using just the tips of your fingers, lightly rub the fat and flour together until you arrive at the consistency of uneven-looking breadcrumbs. Add just a little iced water and mix it in using the knife. When it looks to you as if the mixture is going to stick together, press the dough into a ball with your fingers. Wrap the ball of dough in floured clingfilm and let it sit in the refrigerator for about 30 minutes. This 'resting' will minimize shrinkage when you come to cook the pastry.

### Using a Food Processor

Use the metal blade in the food processor. Sift the flour and salt into the bowl of the processor, add the fats and blend quickly. When the flour and fat are roughly mixed, pour the water slowly and carefully through the funnel, stopping the second the pastry forms a ball. Wrap the pastry in floured clingfilm and let it rest as above.

Shortcrust Pastry

## PASTA

Pasta is a dough in which the liquid used is eggs. The best pasta is made from flour and eggs with no other additions. Even salt should be added to the cooking water rather than to the dough. Although it is comparatively easy these days to buy fresh pasta, the shop-bought kind does not compare in terms of delicacy to the home-made variety, which you might mix, roll out, cut, cook and eat within an hour. This recipe presumes that you have a pasta-rolling machine, which takes the effort out of kneading and with its adjustable rollers will do an efficient job of flattening. It is possible to carry out the whole process by hand but that requires skill and practice. If you are keen on pasta it is worth buying one of the hand-operated machines. It is a game two can play happily.

If you wish to adjust the quantities, remember that one egg will absorb about 4 oz/ 110 g of flour, but the amounts given below will make plenty of fresh pasta for four people and are not unwieldy to handle.

12 oz/340 g plain white flour
3 eggs (size 2)

Heap the flour on to a board and make a well in the centre. The effect should be almost that of a volcano, with a ridge of flour around a central hole. Break the eggs into the well and with a fork gently stir them until the yolks and whites are mixed and then beat them a little faster. Start to bring in the flour from around the inside of the well, using one hand to mix, the other to support the outer wall of flour. Keep going until you have a fairly stiff mixture of eggs and flour. Tumble the rest of the flour on to the egg mixture and, using your hands, press it all together into a ball of dough; then knead it to blend the flour and eggs well together. If the dough seems sticky, dust on a bit of flour and work it in.

### To Roll and Cut the Pasta Dough using a Pasta Machine

Pinch off a piece of dough about the size of a lemon. Put the rest of the dough into a plastic bag to prevent it from drying out. With the rollers at their widest setting, run the dough through them 8 to 10 times, folding it each time between rolls. When it is smooth, shiny and pliable, set the rollers at the next width. Feed the dough into the machine and run it through. Continue down to the narrowest width, which will give you a long thin rectangle of dough. Hang this, with a tea-towel underneath it, over the back of a chair or a broom-handle supported across two chairs or any other suitable contraption. Pinch off another lemon-sized piece of dough and continue as above.

You can cut pasta dough only when it has dried to a certain point when it will fall into separate strands and not stick. About 20 minutes in a warm kitchen will usually do it. So after 20 minutes, go back to your first sheet of dough and see if it seems ready to cut — dry, but not so dry that it snaps. Attach one of the cutting devices to the machine and feed the first sheet of dough through the cutting rollers. Hang the resulting strips back over the tea-towel. Cut the rest of the dough when it is ready in a similar fashion.

### Cooking the Pasta

Bring a large pan of water to the boil. Add a heaped teaspoonful of salt and a teaspoonful of olive oil or vegetable oil. When the water is bubbling enthusiastically, tip in the pasta. Very fresh pasta will take less than a minute to cook. Pasta that has been dried for a day or two will take longer. To test whether it is done, fish out a strand with a wooden fork or spoon, let the hot water drip off and bite the pasta. It should be tender but with just a little resistance to the teeth — what the Italians call *al dente*. Drain the pasta in a large sieve or colander and tip into a warmed serving dish.

# Pasta

1. Mix eggs into flour

2. Press together into a ball

3. Run dough through machine

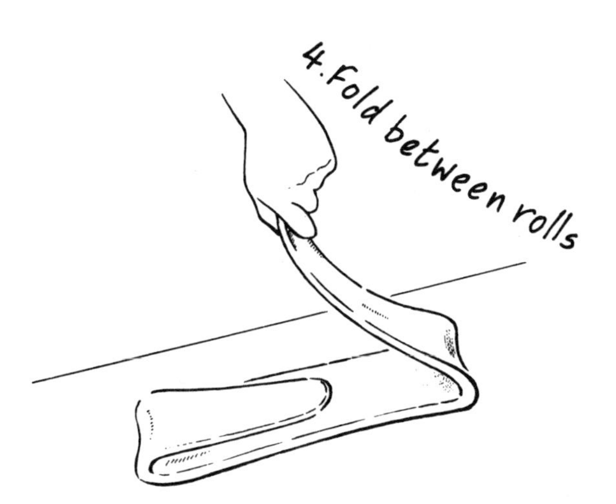

4. Fold between rolls

5. Hang on a broom handle

6. Feed dough through cutting rollers

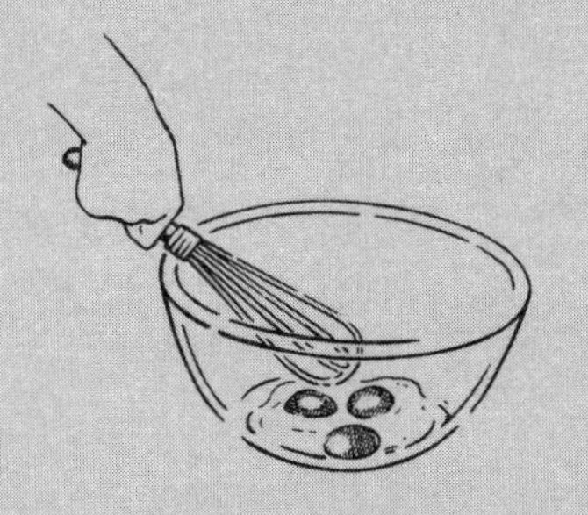

CHAPTER FOUR

# EGGS

BOILED EGGS · SCRAMBLED EGGS

CHINESE SCRAMBLED EGGS · BAKED EGGS

EGGS IN A BUN · ONE-EGG QUICK-FRY OMELETTE

FRENCH OMELETTE · FRENCH TOAST

QUICHE LORRAINE · MAYONNAISE

CHOCOLATE MOUSSE · SOUFFLÉ OMELETTE

SPONGE CAKE · TUILES D'AMANDES

It would be hard to imagine much interesting cooking happening without the presence of eggs. The ability that eggs possess to thicken, in the case of sauces using the yolks, and to lighten, when you are using either the whole egg beaten or egg-whites whipped to a froth, is the reason for much of the magic that takes place in the kitchen. There is something in eggs that pleasingly approaches perfection. For a start they are, quite logically, symbolic of life. The packaging is so elegant and, once understood, their behaviour is so satisfactorily predictable.

To get the most out of eggs — and the possibilities are almost limitless — it is worth observing a few rules:

1. For the most part, eggs need to be heated gently. They start cooking at the relatively low temperature of 158°F/70°C and they cook quickly — an omelette will be ready in 1 to 2 minutes. Overcooking causes the egg proteins to coagulate, resulting in a curdy texture which is only occasionally desirable, e.g. in the case of scrambled eggs — and in order to retain a creaminess, even these should be cooked carefully.

2. Although the matter of the freshness of eggs tends not to be the problem it once was, it is advisable to break each egg into a cup before adding it to your recipe.

3. Egg-whites keep far better than yolks and also freeze well. Some chefs say that defrosted frozen egg-whites make superior meringue (beaten egg-white with sugar).

4. Most egg dishes should be eaten immediately after they are made. Time and soufflés wait for no man.

5. Eggs vary a good deal in size, which in some recipes, particularly those involving baking, will make a significant difference to the result. Where the egg size is given in a recipe, try to keep to it.

6. Salt affects eggs. It liquefies the whites and on the whole is best added at the end of cooking time or, in the case of beating egg-whites, towards the end of the beating process. Never add salt to the water when poaching eggs. A teaspoonful of vinegar instead will help seal the egg-white.

### To Crack an Egg

Have ready a cup or bowl. Hold the egg in one hand and tap the middle of it quite sharply against the edge of the bowl or cup. Pull apart the two halves and let the egg fall into the bowl or cup.

**To Separate an Egg**
Have ready two bowls. Tap the egg as described above and turn the crack uppermost. Pull the egg apart above one of the bowls, holding one half-eggshell upwards like a cup in which sits the yolk. Some of the white will fall into the bowl. Tip the yolk carefully into the other half-eggshell, letting the rest of the white fall into the bowl. Repeat if necessary. Use the sharp edge of the eggshell to separate any white that clings. Put the yolk into the other bowl.

If you are separating several eggs, e.g. for soufflés or meringue, do each one over a small bowl before adding the white to the accumulation of egg-whites in a larger bowl. In that way, if you break one yolk you will not spoil the rest of the egg-whites, which need to be clean of egg-yolk to whisk up successfully. Small scraps of yolk can usually be removed by the use of the edge of a clean eggshell half as a scoop.

**To Whisk Egg-Whites**
It is very important that the bowl and whisk you use for beating egg-whites are clean and free from grease, as any sort of fat or grease will stop the whites foaming. Use a balloon wire whisk, a rotary hand beater or a hand-held electric beater. Food processors and table-top mixers do not give as good results. Start beating the whites and you will see them break into a bubbly mass. Keep beating and they will start to foam and will eventually mount up into snowy peaks. They will reach a point where they are quite stiff and a knife drawn through them will leave a path that doesn't close over. For plain beaten egg-whites, stop at this point and do not overbeat or the foam will start to break down. If you are making meringue, you can add sugar and beat again briefly until you have shiny glistening peaks.

To Separate an Egg

## BOILED EGGS

'He or she can't even boil an egg' is the expression used to describe a completely duff cook. Well, boiling an egg is not a very tricky process, but there are some points to keep in mind. The cooking time will determine the consistency of the white and the yolk and the cooking temperature will also affect the final result. The water for boiling eggs should not seethe and bubble fiercely, as this introduces the risk of the eggs cracking through bashing against each other and the side of the pan.

Bring a pan of water to just below the boil. With the help of a ladle or small sieve, lower in the eggs and release them carefully. For soft-boiled eggs with the whites solid and the yolks liquid, let them cook for 3 to 5 minutes (a large egg taking longer than a small one). If the eggs are very cold, i.e. straight from the refrigerator, it is safer (to avoid cracking) to start them in cold water, bring the water to a simmer and time them as above.

For a hard-boiled egg to eat hot, let it simmer for 6 to 7 minutes, and for a hard-boiled egg that you will cool and eat cold, let it simmer for 15 minutes or more. Keeping the water at no more than a simmer will ensure that the whites do not harden excessively and get tough. To cool hard-boiled eggs, run cold water into the pan until the water is quite cold and tap the shells of the eggs against the side of the pan to crack them. Let them sit in the cold water for a few minutes. This technique minimizes the possibility of the egg-yolk having a greenish-grey rim and helps ensure smooth peeling. The fresher the egg, the harder it is to peel smoothly.

## SCRAMBLED EGGS

Scrambled eggs and omelettes are both made by a process of mixing the yolks and whites together, but in the case of scrambled eggs the blending is done in a much more casual way as, contrary to that in most other cooking, your aim is a lumpy texture. It is not worth scrambling fewer than three eggs. The eggs must be cooked very gently to prevent them from drying out.

Serves 2–3

5 or 6 eggs
2 oz/55 g butter
salt and pepper

Break the eggs into a bowl. Take half the butter and cut it into small pieces. Add these to the eggs. Beat with a fork until the yolks and whites are only just amalgamated. Season with a good pinch of salt and pepper. Heat the remaining butter over a low heat in a heavy-bottomed, preferably non-stick saucepan. When it is melted and just starting to foam, add the eggs. Using a wooden spoon, keep stirring gently, breaking up the eggs as they begin to coagulate but leaving them quite lumpy. As they cook, the small pieces of butter will melt and help keep the eggs moist. When the eggs are just set but still shiny and glistening, remove them from the heat, remembering that the heat of the pan will continue to cook them. Pile on to hot toast or warm plates.

Note: Some recipes tell you to add a little milk to the eggs. However, the flavour of butter alone is much nicer, and with the addition of milk, the slightest overcooking will separate the eggs from the liquid — a curds-and-whey effect — and spoil the result.

## CHINESE SCRAMBLED EGGS

Eggs scrambled in vegetable oil have a very different flavour and, it must be said, a rather healthier aspect. A wok is the ideal pan for cooking this dish, but it can also be prepared in a large frying pan. The recipe below suggests chives or spring onions as an ingredient, but the same method can be used when any of a variety of ingredients — such as a selection from thinly cut vegetables, minced pork, prawns and finely sliced chicken — are stir-fried and cooked before the eggs are added. If you like a little hotness about your food, thread-like slices of fresh green chilli go surprisingly well in eggs.

Serves 2–3

1 bunch chives weighing about 2 oz/55 g *or* 1 bunch spring onions
4 eggs (size 1 or 2)
3 tbsp vegetable oil
pinch of salt and pepper

*To serve alongside*
2 tbsp soy sauce
pinch of sugar
1 tsp vegetable oil or sesame oil

Mix together the soy sauce, sugar and oil and pour into a small shallow dish. Trim the chives and cut them into ½-in/1-cm lengths, or clean the spring onions by cutting off the roots and the top parts, leaving about 1-in/2.5-cm dark green stalks, and peeling off the outer skin. Chop these like the chives. Beat the eggs in a mixing bowl with 1 tablespoonful of the oil. Season with salt and pepper and beat again. Heat the remaining oil in a wok or frying pan and when it is hot, add the chives or onions or any other ingredients that you have chosen (see above). Stir the chives or spring onions around for about 20 seconds (more substantial ingredients will take longer) and then pour in the egg. Using a wok scoop or metal spatula, keep lifting and turning the eggs to blend them with the oil and chives. When all the egg has set, serve immediately on warm plates with the dipping sauce alongside.

## BAKED EGGS

Of the many ways of cooking eggs, baking them in the oven is often overlooked, but baked eggs have their own special flavour and seem more serious, less of a snack than, say, fried eggs. Eggs can be baked in small ovenproof dishes — sometimes called ramekins — or in edible containers such as bread rolls, which is an elegant idea detailed below in the recipe for Eggs in a Bun.

Baking eggs gives you the opportunity to slip beneath them a good surprise such as a small slice of ham, some fried mushrooms or a spoonful of the jelly that sets from the juices of roast meat (in the case of beef, the dark jelly that underlines beef dripping), but just with butter, cream and maybe a few fresh herbs as suggested below they are delicious.

Makes 4

4 eggs
salt and pepper
1 tbsp chopped fresh herbs such as parsley or chives
4 tsp single cream
1 oz/30 g butter

Turn on the oven to 350°F/180°C/gas mark 4.

Divide the butter between four small ovenproof dishes such as cocotte dishes or ramekins. Stout cups will do. Fill a roasting pan or other oven tin with hot water to come half-way up the dishes or cups. This makes what is called a *bain-marie* and cooking in this water jacket ensures that the contents do not dry out.

Put the small dishes into the hot water. Break an egg into each dish and season with salt and pepper. Add a teaspoonful of cream to each egg. Bake in the oven for 12 minutes. Remove them very carefully and remember that the eggs will go on cooking a little bit in their hot containers.

You can also cook the eggs on top of the stove in a pan half-filled with hot water. Use a wide shallow saucepan with a cover for the *bain-marie*. Place the individual egg dishes in this and simmer the water gently for 7 to 9 minutes with the saucepan lid on.

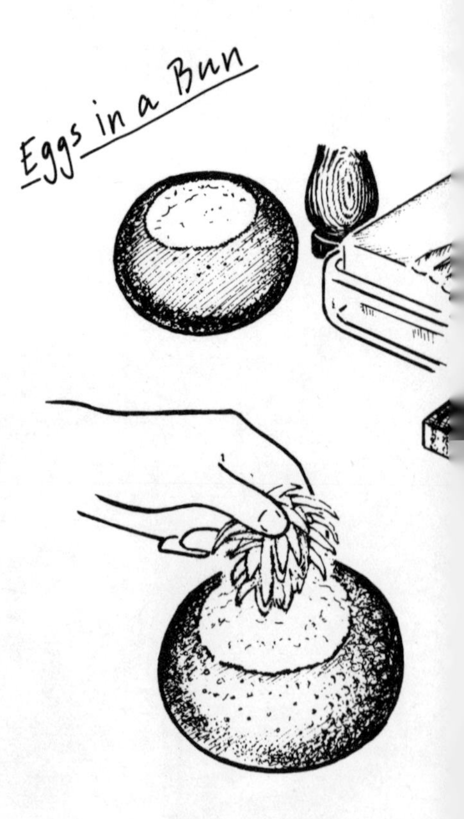

## EGGS IN A BUN

Makes 4

4 round bread rolls
2 oz/55 g butter
2 oz/55 g grated hard cheese, e.g. Cheddar
4 eggs
salt and pepper

Turn on the oven to 350°F/180°C/gas mark 4.

Cut the tops off the buns and carefully pull out the soft insides. Butter the insides of the rolls and set them in the oven for 5 minutes to crisp. Remove them, set aside half the grated cheese and put the rest inside the buns. Separate the eggs, putting the whites into a large bowl and each yolk into a bun. Season each egg-yolk with salt and pepper. Turn up the oven to 400°F/200°C/gas mark 6.

Whisk the egg-whites until they are stiff and snowy. Fold in the rest of the grated cheese and spoon the mixture on top of the yolks. Put back in the oven and bake for 12 minutes.

## ONE-EGG QUICK-FRY OMELETTE

There is a good deal of mystique attached to making omelettes, with some people being admired for having a natural talent for it. The omelette in the recipe below needs no god-given gifts and the way it rises in the pan is always dramatic and praiseworthy. It makes a quick snack and is an ideal accompaniment, particularly in its curried form, to the Stir-Fried Vegetables in Chapter Seven.

1 egg per person
salt and pepper
1 tbsp vegetable oil per person

Cook one omelette at a time.

Break the egg into a small mixing bowl. Add a pinch of salt and pepper and, using a fork, beat the egg vigorously until it is well mixed and frothy.

Heat the oil in a small frying pan until it is very hot but not smoking. Give the egg a final whisk and pour it into the frying pan. It will puff up quite dramatically. Turn it over and it will puff up some more. Serve immediately.

### Curried omelette

If you like the flavour of spices, add 1 level teaspoonful of curry powder to the oil in the pan and let it heat up with the oil. Fry the omelette as above.

French Omelette

## FRENCH OMELETTE

This recipe is for the more conventional omelette that rolls well round various fillings such as grated cheese, diced ham, fried chopped bacon, sautéd mushrooms or chopped seasoned tomato. With a bit of practice you will soon learn how to make an omelette that is light and layered and juicy inside. It is important to have a non-stick or well-seasoned heavy-bottomed frying pan.

3 eggs
salt and pepper
1 dsp finely chopped fresh parsley (optional)
2 tsp cold water
½ oz/15 g butter

Break the eggs into a bowl and add a pinch of salt and pepper, parsley if you have it and the water which helps lighten the mixture. Whisk with a fork or wire whisk until well amalgamated. Melt the butter in a frying pan over a medium heat and when the butter froths, pour in the eggs.

Let the eggs just set on the bottom and then, using a metal spatula, lift one corner of the eggs and let some of the wet egg mixture run beneath. Do this several times at different points of the circumference of the omelette, building up a layered effect. When the surface of the omelette is still glistening but there is no mixture running freely, add your choice of filling (or leave the omelette plain). Using the spatula, flick one side of the omelette to the centre and then, holding the pan with a cloth or oven glove, roll the omelette out on to a warm plate.

## FRENCH TOAST

This is an ideal quick and nutritious snack.

2 slices bread, brown or white, about ½ in/1 cm thick
1 egg
salt and pepper
1 oz/30 g butter or mixture of butter and oil, for frying

Break the egg into a shallow soup plate. Add a pinch of salt and pepper. Beat with a fork until the egg is frothy. Soak the bread (you may have to do it a slice at a time) in the egg. Melt the butter or butter and oil in a frying pan. When the fat is hot, fry the bread on one side and then on the other.

To make a sweet version, omit the salt and pepper from the egg, and when you take the toast from the pan, while it is still hot, sprinkle with a mixture of two teaspoonfuls of sugar mixed with half a teaspoonful of ground cinnamon.

## QUICHE LORRAINE OR EGG AND BACON TART

A quiche ably demonstrates the ability of eggs to set a liquid to a firm custard. It is the combining of eggs with milk and/or cream that enables the egg proteins to gel. Although it is easy to overcook a sweet creamy custard made on top of the stove, it is hard to go wrong with a quiche filling, and once the principle is understood the variations are many. In place of bacon as the main flavouring ingredient — or with it — you can use cheese and onions, leeks, tomatoes or mushrooms. In quiches lie many ideas for savoury vegetarian dishes.

Serves 3–4

half the amount of Shortcrust Pastry given in the recipe in Chapter Three (p.38)
3 eggs
½ pint/290 ml single cream
½ oz/15 g butter
4–6 rashers bacon
2 oz/55 g grated hard cheese, e.g. Cheddar or Gruyère
salt and pepper

Roll the pastry thinly and line a pie tin about 8 in/20 cm in diameter. Set in the refrigerator to chill for about 30 minutes. This helps reduce shrinkage of the pastry when it is baked.

Set the oven to 400°F/200°C/gas mark 6. Cover the bottom of the pastry with foil and put on a handful of dried peas or beans. Bake in the oven for 15 minutes. This is called 'baking blind', and the foil and beans (which you should keep to use again for the same purpose) stop the pastry puffing up when it is pre-cooked. Remove the tin from the oven and lower the temperature of the oven to 375°F/190°C/gas mark 5.

Beat together the eggs and cream and season with salt and pepper, keeping in mind the saltiness of the bacon. Cut the bacon into 1-in/2.5-cm lengths and fry in the butter until cooked but not browned. Sprinkle the bacon and half the cheese over the pastry (from which you have removed the foil and baking beans). Pour on the egg mixture. Sprinkle on the remaining cheese and bake for 35 minutes. Eat hot, warm or cold. Warm is nicest.

## MAYONNAISE

Mayonnaise is an emulsion, a mixture in which fat (oil) is dispersed in water (a constituent of egg-yolk) and which achieves thickness and cohesion partly owing to other ingredients in the egg-yolk such as lecithin. Making mayonnaise by hand is a revelation in the chemistry of cooking and much that is technical and scientific could be written here about why and how mayonnaise reaches its creamy texture. It is enough now to observe a few rules in order to prevent mayonnaise — which has a reputation for fickleness — from separating back into its original parts.

1. Use egg-yolks, oil and implements at room temperature.

2. Mayonnaise can be made with one egg-yolk, while using two is more reliable, but that doesn't mean that using three is foolproof; three yolks contribute too much water to the mixture.

3. Oil is added to water rather than the other way round, and the smaller the initial amount of oil added, the easier it is to divide it into the necessary microscopic droplets and coat them with the emulsifying agent.

4. Once about the same amount of oil as there is egg-yolk has been added, the oil can be poured in with slightly less care and precision.

5. Mayonnaise should not be stored in cold (refrigerator) or too warm conditions.

6. If you are using a food processor, start with a whole egg, as the albumen proteins help stabilize the mixture when it is subjected to the vigour and heat of the motor-driven blades.

7. Have a go. It's immensely satisfactory!

2 egg-yolks (size 2)
½ pint/290 ml olive oil or vegetable oil or a mixture
2 tsp lemon juice or wine vinegar
salt and pepper

Put the egg-yolks in a medium-sized mixing bowl. Stir them vigorously with a wooden spoon, and when they are well mixed, add a drop of oil. When that is mixed in, add another few drops of oil, stir some more and continue in this fashion until the mixture looks reliably thickened and at least two tablespoonfuls of oil have been added. You can now add oil more freely, stirring all the while. When all the oil has been added, the mixture should be thick with the look and texture almost of an ointment. Add the lemon juice or wine vinegar and a pinch of

salt and pepper. Stir, and then taste to see if the mayonnaise needs more seasoning.

Note: Should the mayonnaise fail to thicken or should it separate, place another egg-yolk in a clean bowl, stir it with a clean wooden spoon and add the separated mixture bit by tiny bit until it is clear that the mixture has thickened. Then add the rest of the mixture more slap-happily.

## MAKING MAYONNAISE IN A FOOD PROCESSOR

1 whole egg (size 1 or 2)
½ pint/290 ml olive oil or vegetable oil or a mixture
2 tsp lemon juice or wine vinegar
salt and pepper

Use the metal or the plastic blade in the food processor. Break the egg into the bowl of the processor and whizz it for 30 seconds. Slowly pour the oil through the spout while the machine is switched on. By the time all the oil has been added, the mayonnaise will be thick and pale in colour. Add the seasonings, whizz again and taste to see if more are needed.

## AIOLI OR GARLIC MAYONNAISE

If you like the flavour and punchiness of garlic, this makes an excellent dip for raw vegetables and quarters of hard-boiled egg or a sauce for cold fish or meat. Stir one or two crushed cloves of garlic and a teaspoonful of French mustard into the egg-yolks and add oil as for regular mayonnaise.

## CHOCOLATE MOUSSE

The simpler the better is the rule with this most delectable of desserts. The beaten egg-whites lighten it and the chocolate sets it. It is a mousse that needs no gelatine.

Serves 4

4 oz/110–125 g plain chocolate
4 eggs (size 2 or 3)
1 dsp instant coffee

Break up the chocolate into squares. Put them either into a bowl that fits over a saucepan without touching its base or into the top part of a double boiler. Place the coffee in a cup and half-fill with boiling water. Put three tablespoonfuls of the made-up coffee in with the chocolate. Put hot water into the saucepan or bottom half of the double boiler and set on a low heat. Let the chocolate melt very gently above it. The slower it melts the better, as too much heat applied can make it grainy. When the chocolate has completely melted (it can do so without losing the square shapes), remove from the heat and stir to blend the coffee and chocolate.

Separate the eggs, putting the whites in a large clean bowl. Add the yolks one by one to the chocolate mixture, beating them in with a wooden spoon. With a hand-held rotary whisk or hand-held electric beater, beat the egg-whites until they form firm snowy peaks. Using a metal spoon, fold a quarter of the egg-whites into the chocolate mixture, taking care to maintain the spongy texture of the whites. Pour this on to the remaining egg-whites in the large bowl and fold the two mixtures together gently. Take care that no little white 'islands' of egg-white remain, but mix only as much as is absolutely necessary. Divide between small ramekins or pretty cups or glasses and chill in the refrigerator for a few hours before serving.

1. Heat chocolate

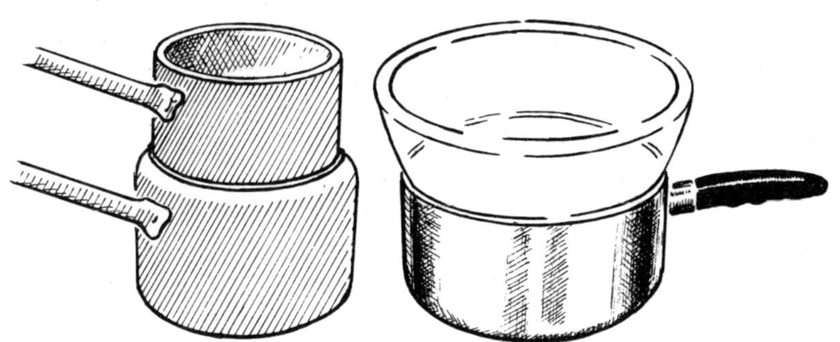

Double boiler or bowl & saucepan

## SOUFFLÉ OMELETTE

A quite different effect in omelettes is achieved when the eggs are separated and the yolks folded into the stiffly beaten whites. The result is an instant soufflé made in a frying pan, a wonderful finish to a meal.

Serves 2

4 eggs
2 tbsp cold water
1 tsp caster sugar
½ oz/15 g butter
1½ tbsp jam of your choice

Warm two plates and a serving dish. Warm the jam gently in a small pan over a low heat. Separate the eggs, putting the yolks in a medium-sized bowl and the whites in a larger one. Beat the egg-yolks with the water and sugar. Whisk the egg-whites until stiff and snowy. Pour on the yolk mixture and fold it in carefully with a metal spoon. Heat the butter in an omelette pan until it is foaming and just starting to turn golden. Turn down the heat and pour in the egg mixture. Do not stir, just let the mixture become puffy until small bubbles start to burst on the surface. Spoon the warmed jam on to the omelette, fold it over and slide it on to the warmed serving plate. Sprinkle with a little sugar. Divide and eat immediately.

## SPONGE CAKE

One of the most popular roles for the versatile egg is the lightening and leavening of sponge cake. This basic sponge can be used for a layer cake or to make small fairy cakes cooked in paper cases or a bun tin.

4 oz/110 g caster sugar
4 oz/110 g butter
4 oz/110 g self-raising flour *or* 4 oz/110 g plain flour sifted with 1½ tsp baking powder
2 eggs
a little extra butter and flour, for preparing tins

Turn on the oven to 375°F/190°C/gas mark 5.

Lightly butter and flour two 8-in/20-cm cake tins. Using a wooden spoon, beat together the butter and sugar until white and creamy. Beat the two eggs in a separate bowl. Then beat the eggs into the butter and sugar mixture a little at a time. Fold in the sifted flour. Spread half the mixture in each tin as lightly as possible. Bake in the top half of the oven for 20 minutes — without opening the oven door to peek. Take the tins out of the oven and cool them on a wire rack. Run a knife around the edges of the cakes and turn out. Sandwich the two together with jam and/or whipped cream.

### Using a Food Processor

With the metal blade of the food processor fitted, whizz together the butter and sugar until the mixture is light and fluffy. Add the eggs one at a time, giving a whizz after each addition. Add the flour and blend for seconds, long enough only to mix in the flour. Do not over-process. Finish as above.

## TUILES D'AMANDES OR ALMOND TILES

Some recipes, such as the one for mayonnaise, leave you with spare egg-whites. Here is a quick, easy and profitable (to your taste-buds) way of using them up to make crisp, seductive biscuits.

Makes about 18 biscuits

2 oz/55 g butter
2 egg-whites
4 oz/100–125 g caster sugar
2 oz/55 g plain flour
1 oz/30 g flaked almonds
extra butter, for greasing baking sheets

Turn on the oven to 350°F/180°C/gas mark 4.

Grease baking sheets with a little butter rubbed on with kitchen paper. Place the 2 oz/55 g of butter in a small glass or china mixing bowl and set that over a saucepan of hot water. Simmer the water until the butter has melted but has not become hot. Set the bowl aside. Put the egg-whites (perhaps those left over from making mayonnaise) into a large clean bowl. Add the sugar and mix together with a fork. Sift in the flour and mix that in. Then add the almonds and melted butter and give it all a good stir. Drop teaspoonfuls of the mixture on to the prepared baking sheets, leaving gaps of about 5 in/13 cm between them. Bake for 7 or 8 minutes or until well spread and a light gold colour. Remove the baking trays from the oven and let them sit for a minute. Using a palette knife, lift the biscuits off the tray and drape each one either over the side of a bottle or a rolling pin, so that it will set slightly curved to give a 'tile' effect, or over the bottom of a small up-turned glass to make a biscuit basket for ice-cream, sorbet or fruit.

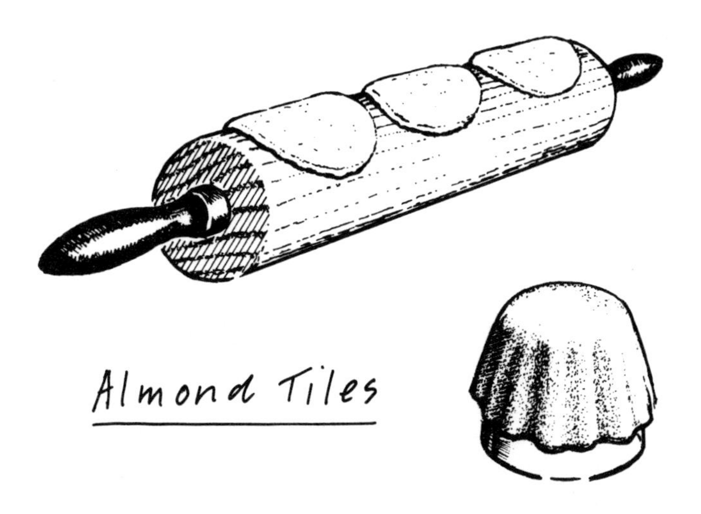

Almond Tiles

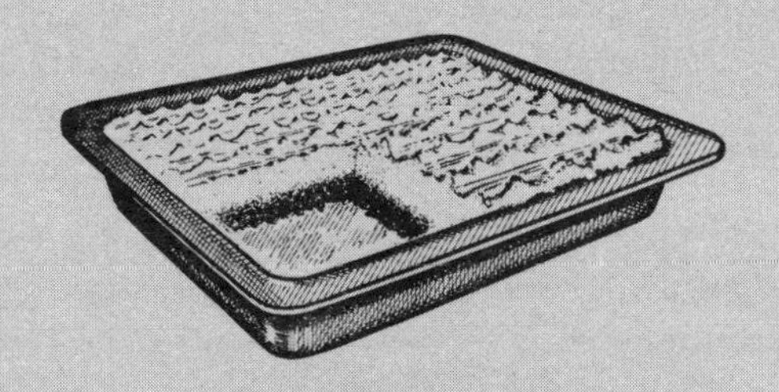

CHAPTER FIVE

# CASSEROLES

SPAGHETTI BOLOGNESE · SHEPHERD'S PIE

MOUSSAKA · CHILLI CON CARNE

GOULASH · IRISH STEW · FISH PIE

BLACK-EYED BEAN AND VEGETABLE CASSEROLE

CHICKEN CASSEROLE

has a comforting
, of a warm, welcoming,
sic and, on the whole,
ooking. Most casseroles use
and the cheaper cuts of meat
or fi... gh results can be very
different ... hod tends to follow a pattern.
The main meat ingredient is trimmed to size, then browned, seasoned, moistened and tenderized. Casseroles can be made ahead of time and often benefit from being heated up a day later.

Slow cooking is usually appropriate for making casseroles, and they can be simmered either in the oven or on top of the stove. Frequently the cooking pot is also the serving dish, making a casserole an easy, efficient meal often complete in itself or needing only bread, potatoes, rice or noodles as an accompaniment.

The first ingredient that we are dealing with, minced meat, can also be cooked quickly, as in hamburgers or meatballs, but minced meat simmered with vegetables, stock, flavourings and spices is the jumping-off point for an impressive number of dishes. The sauce in the recipe for Spaghetti Bolognese below can be adapted to be used in making Shepherd's Pie, Chilli con Carne and Moussaka, and its preparation demonstrates most of the steps of casserole cooking: the softening of vegetables for flavour, the sealing or browning of the meat, the addition of liquid for sauce and the simmering for tenderness and togetherness.

## SPAGHETTI BOLOGNESE

Serves 4–5

1 large or 2 medium-sized onions, peeled and finely chopped
2 large carrots, peeled and finely chopped
1 large clove of garlic or 2 small ones, peeled and finely chopped or pushed through a garlic press
2 tbsp vegetable oil or olive oil
12 oz/340 g minced beef
1 glass (⅓ pint/100 ml) milk
1 x 14 oz/400 g can of peeled tomatoes
1 generous tbsp tomato paste
½ pint/290 ml stock or left-over wine if there is any around or a mixture of both
1 tsp dried oregano
salt and pepper

1 lb/450 g spaghetti
1 dsp vegetable oil
salt

2 oz/55 g grated Parmesan cheese

In a large frying pan heat up the oil. Fry the onions, carrots and garlic quite gently for about 5 minutes or until they are softened. Add the minced beef and fry, stirring, until the meat is browned all over. Pour in the milk, turn up the heat and bubble the mixture until the milk seems to have cooked away. This sweetens and tenderizes the meat. Add the tomatoes and tomato paste and stir to dissolve the paste and break up the tomatoes. Simmer for 5 minutes and then add the stock or wine or a mixture of both, the oregano and a good pinch of salt and pepper. Simmer for as long as you have time, the longer the better. If you have not much time, bubble the mixture to reduce the sauce. Taste, and add extra seasoning if necessary. Sometimes tinned tomatoes need a pinch of sugar. Add this if you think it a good idea.

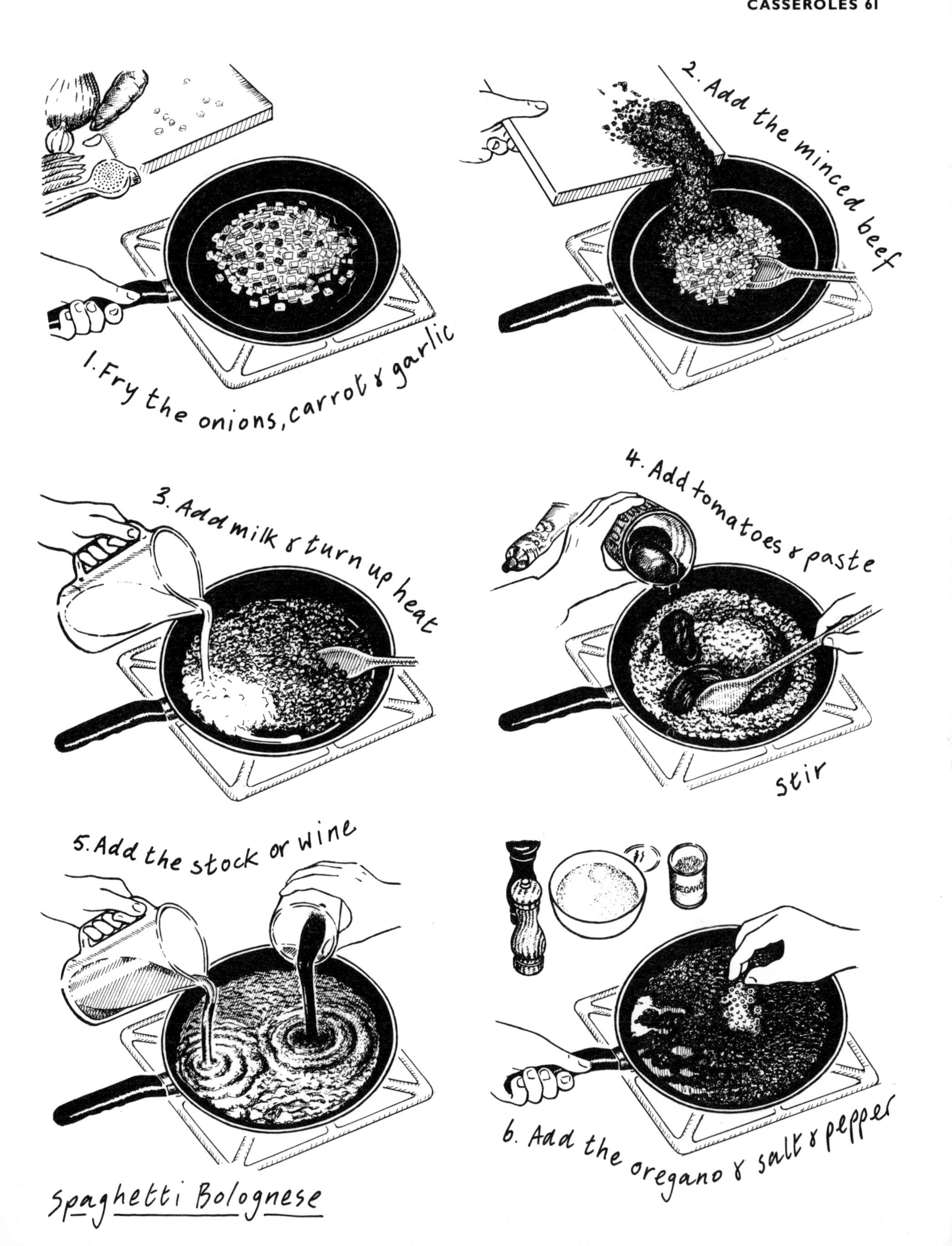
1. Fry the onions, carrot & garlic
2. Add the minced beef
3. Add milk & turn up heat
4. Add tomatoes & paste
stir
5. Add the stock or wine
6. Add the oregano & salt & pepper
OREGANO
Spaghetti Bolognese

Bring a large pan of water to the boil. Add the oil and a hefty pinch of salt. Push the spaghetti into the pan — it will bend after contact with the boiling water, enabling you to coil long strands into the pan. Start testing to see if it is ready after about 8 minutes. Fish out a strand of pasta with a long-handled fork, let it drain and bite it. You want the pasta only just soft, still with a little resistance to the teeth, what the Italians term *al dente*. When it reaches that point, pour the contents of the pan into a colander and let the water drain away. Return the spaghetti to the pan or tip it into a heated serving dish. Serve the spaghetti with the sauce and offer grated Parmesan cheese separately.

## SHEPHERD'S PIE

Serves 4–5

**Base**

meat sauce as for Spaghetti Bolognese above

**Topping**

2 lb/900 g potatoes
2 tbsp hot milk
1 oz/30 g butter
salt and pepper
ground nutmeg (optional)
a little extra butter

Make the meat sauce as for Spaghetti Bolognese and simmer until most of the liquid has evaporated. Peel the potatoes. Put them in a large pan of water, add a teaspoonful of salt, bring to the boil and cook for 15 to 20 minutes or until so well done they are practically falling apart. Pour into a sieve or colander set in the sink and drain them rather carelessly, as a little bit of waterlogging helps to promote lightness. Return them to the pan over a low heat and mash with a fork or potato-masher. Add the hot milk and mash some more. Blend in the butter and stir or mash until melted. Season with more salt if needed, some pepper and a pinch of nutmeg if you like the taste.

Turn on the oven to 400°F/200°C/gas mark 6.

Tip the meat mixture into a pie dish. Let it cool slightly and then carefully spread the mashed potato over the top. Rough up the surface with a fork. Dot a little more butter around the mash. Place in the oven for 20 to 30 minutes, by which time the potato topping should be tipped with gold.

## MOUSSAKA

Serves 4–5

### Base

meat sauce from the recipe for Spaghetti Bolognese, made with minced beef or lamb and seasoned with a pinch of ground cinnamon in addition
1 medium-sized aubergine
salt
vegetable oil, for frying aubergine

### Topping

see recipe in Chapter Two (p.27)

Wipe the aubergine with a damp cloth. Trim it at both ends and slice it into pieces about ¼ in/0.5 cm thick. Sprinkle the slices with salt and leave them while you make up the meat sauce from the Spaghetti Bolognese recipe, adding a pinch of cinnamon when you fry the meat. Moussaka in Greece or Cyprus would most probably be made with lamb and if you can buy minced lamb or have enough left-over roast lamb to mince, it is both good and authentic.

Salting the aubergine slices causes them to 'sweat' and removes any bitter taste. Using kitchen paper, wipe the aubergine slices dry. In a large shallow frying pan, heat up enough vegetable oil to come ½ in/1 cm up the inside of the pan. When the oil is hot, fry the aubergine slices, turning once, and put them to drain on kitchen paper.

Make the moussaka topping as in the recipe in Chapter Two.

Turn on the oven to 375°F/190°C/gas mark 5.

Put half the meat into a small ovenproof casserole. Make a layer using half the aubergine slices. Add the rest of the meat and cover with the remaining aubergine slices. Cover with the moussaka topping and bake for 35 minutes by which time the top will be puffed and golden brown.

## CHILLI CON CARNE

Which is the correct recipe for chilli causes heated arguments among its fans, the force of discussion probably directly related to the amount of chilli used to spike the mixture. Since there are so many approaches to making chilli, this one is no more or less authentic than others. Judge the amount of chilli powder by how hot you like your food, bearing in mind that one teaspoonful will give a mild result. Boiled rice goes well with chilli.

Serves 4–5

meat sauce from the recipe for Spaghetti Bolognese
1–3 tsp chilli powder
½ tsp ground cumin (optional but desirable)
1 tsp dried oregano
1 x 14 oz/400 g tin of red kidney beans

Make the meat sauce from the Spaghetti Bolognese recipe, adding the chilli powder, ground cumin and oregano just after you have fried the onions, carrots and garlic, stirring the herbs and spices around to cook for a minute or two before adding the minced beef. When the sauce is cooked, open the tin of kidney beans, drain them in a sieve held over the sink and add them to the meat mixture. Stir gently and simmer for 5 more minutes to heat the beans through.

## GOULASH

Goulash (*gulyás*) is a Hungarian casserole — sometimes as much a soup as a stew — that uses paprika for flavour and colouring. Paprika can be hot, but the kind exported for sale in this country is usually mild, almost sweet, so that quite a lot can, and should, be used. Since paprika is in fact a vegetable, when it is used in cooking it is not fried like a spice — as it is easy to burn it — but added as an ingredient. Goulash is a stew that uses no flour — the paprika contributes to the thickening of the sauce. Lard is the cooking fat that gives the richest and most authentic result.

Serves 4–5

1½ lb/700 g stewing beef
¾ lb/340 g onions
2 cloves of garlic
2 tbsp lard or vegetable oil
3 carrots
2 level tbsp paprika
1 tsp caraway seeds (optional)
1 lb/450 g potatoes
salt and pepper
1½–2 pints/850 ml–1 litre water (depending on how soupy you want it)

Cut the beef into cubes, trimming off any obvious fat. Peel and chop the onions and garlic. Peel the carrots and chop them into quite large chunks. Melt the lard or heat the oil in a sturdy casserole and fry the onions and garlic gently. When they are a golden brown, add the beef and stir it around, turning it, until it is lightly browned. Take the pot from the stove and stir in the paprika. Pour in the water and add the carrots and caraway seeds if you like the flavour. Return to the heat, bring to a simmer and add salt and pepper to taste. Cook gently for an hour or until the meat is tender. After the hour, peel the potatoes and cut them into cubes the same size as the beef. Add them to the stew and cook for a further half-hour.

If you want to make a really hearty meal, you could add dumplings towards the end of the cooking time, following the instructions for Dumplings in Chapter Three (p.35).

## IRISH STEW

Irish Stew and Lancashire Hot-Pot have much in common, namely lamb, onions and potatoes as the main ingredients. This is a very simple and economical but rewarding dish to make. The thinly sliced potatoes thicken the stew, the thicker ones form a crust on top.

Serves 4–5

2½ lb/1 kg middle neck of lamb or other stewing lamb
2 lb/900 g potatoes (about 6 medium-sized ones)
1 lb/450 g onions
salt and pepper
¾ pint/450 ml water or veal, beef or chicken stock
1 heaped tbsp fresh chopped parsley

Trim the meat of fat and keep the fat to one side. Peel the onions and slice them thinly. Peel the potatoes. Slice half of them thinly, about ¼ in/0.5 cm thick, and the rest a little bit thicker, about ½ in/1 cm. Melt the fat trimmings in a heavy frying pan and brown the meat. Remove it and fry the onions until soft and turning golden. Put a layer of thinly sliced potatoes in the bottom of a casserole dish. Next put a layer of onions and then a layer of meat. Season with salt and pepper. Repeat, finishing the layering with the thicker potatoes. Add the water or stock and bring the contents of the casserole to a simmer. Cover and cook for 1½ to 2 hours. Alternatively, bring the casserole to a simmer and cook for the same amount of time in a low oven, 300°F/150°C/gas mark 2. Sprinkle with parsley before serving.

## FISH PIE

When making fish pie it is a good idea to use a combination of fish that provides a contrast, such as white fish and smoked fish or white fish and shellfish. No accusations of monotony or do-goodishness can then be levelled at it. Carefully made it is a lovely dish.

Serves 4–5

½ lb/225 g white fish such as cod, haddock or whiting
½ lb/225 g smoked fish such as haddock or cod
a few peeled prawns if possible
3 eggs
Basic White Sauce from the recipe in Chapter Two, using the milk the fish is cooked in as the liquid
1 tbsp chopped fresh parsley
mashed potatoes from the Shepherd's Pie recipe in this chapter

Turn on the oven to 350°F/180°C/gas mark 4.

Put the fish (but not the prawns) in a shallow ovenproof dish and pour on the ½ pint/290 ml of milk from the Basic White Sauce recipe. Cook the fish in the oven for about 20 minutes. Remove the dish from the oven, remove the fish from the milk and leave on a plate to cool. Put on the eggs to boil. Make up the white sauce using the milk the fish has cooked in, plus any that drains from the fish on to the plate, plus a bit more (or a dash of white wine if this is handy) if you need it to get the sauce to the consistency of thick cream. When the eggs have boiled for 10 minutes, remove the pan from the stove and run cold water into it until all the water is cold. Bash the eggs against the side of the pan, leave for a few minutes in the cold water and then peel. Cut the eggs in half and then each half into two lengthwise. Remove any skin from the fish and break the fish up into chunks or flakes. Mix the fish, eggs, prawns if you have them and parsley into the white sauce. Taste for seasoning and add more salt and pepper if needed. Pile the mixture into a pie dish and cover it with mashed potato. Make a wavy pattern with a fork. Dot with butter. Turn up the oven to 450°F/230°C/gas mark 8 and heat the pie through for 10 minutes, browning the crests of the mashed potatoes.

## BLACK-EYED BEAN AND VEGETABLE CASSEROLE

Delicious, cheap and beneficial vegetable casseroles can be made using dried beans and a mixture of root and other vegetables. Black-eyed beans are one of the quickest types of dried beans to cook. White haricot beans and red kidney beans need more soaking time.

Serves 4

8 oz/225 g black-eyed beans
1 large onion, peeled and chopped
3 carrots, peeled and chopped
3 sticks celery, cleaned, de-stringed and chopped
1 green pepper
2 cloves of garlic, peeled and chopped or crushed
1 oz/30 g butter
1 tbsp olive oil or vegetable oil
1 x 14 oz/400 g can of peeled tomatoes
1 tbsp tomato purée
1 tbsp wine vinegar or a glass of left-over red wine
salt and pepper
pinch of sugar

Wash the beans, removing any dust or foreign bodies. Put them in a pan. Add cold water to cover well and bring to the boil. Take the pan off the heat, cover it and let the beans sit for 20 minutes or longer. Drain, cover with fresh water and bring to a simmer. Depending on the age of the beans, they should now cook in half an hour or less or more. In any case the pre-cooking will cut down on cooking time. When the beans are tender, drain them.

Cut the green pepper in half. Remove the seeds, any stringy parts and the stalk. Slice the two halves into thin strips or squares depending on your preference. Melt the butter and oil in a casserole that will hold everything and lightly fry all the prepared vegetables including the garlic. They should soften but not brown. Stir in the cooked black-eyed beans. Add the tomato purée and stir around, then add the vinegar or wine and the tinned tomatoes. Bring the mixture to a simmer. Add salt, pepper and sugar. The last helps to bring out the flavour of tinned tomatoes. Let the casserole cook for about 30 minutes. Taste for seasoning and add more if necessary.

## CHICKEN CASSEROLE

This simple chicken dish follows most of the usual steps involved in making a casserole. The meat is floured, then fried and browned with ingredients such as onion and bacon added for flavour, then moistened with stock and cooked to tenderness. Once you have mastered the idea you can add other ingredients that take your fancy. Chicken takes less time to cook then red stewing meat.

Serves 4–5

3 lb/1.35 kg roasting chicken
1½ tbsp plain white flour
salt and pepper
1½ oz/45 g butter
1 tbsp olive oil
4 rashers bacon, cut into ½-in/1-cm pieces
1 large onion, peeled and finely chopped
1 clove of garlic, peeled and crushed
1 pint/570 ml stock made from stock cube + 1 glass white wine (optional)
4 oz/110 g button mushrooms, cut in half
1–2 tbsp finely chopped parsley
2 slices bread, brown or white
1 oz/30 g butter + 1 dsp vegetable or olive oil, for frying bread

Joint the chicken and trim the pieces of any fat or overhanging bits of skin. Spoon the flour into a shallow soup plate and season with salt and pepper. Roll the pieces of chicken in the flour until they are lightly covered. Heat half of the butter and olive oil in a casserole and fry the bacon, onion and garlic gently. When they are softened and the fat is running from the bacon, add the chicken pieces and fry them, turning until lightly browned all over. Add the stock and wine if you have some and bring the liquid to a simmer. Cover the pan and cook gently on top of the stove for an hour. Ten minutes before the chicken will be ready, sauté the mushrooms in the other half of the butter until they are softened. Add them (but not their juices) to the casserole. Cut the slices of bread into triangles. Fry them in the butter and oil until brown and crisp. Drain on kitchen paper. Dip one corner of each slice of bread into the finely chopped parsley and tuck the opposite edge into the chicken casserole around the edge. Sprinkle any remaining parsley over the casserole and serve. Rice or noodles are a good accompaniment.

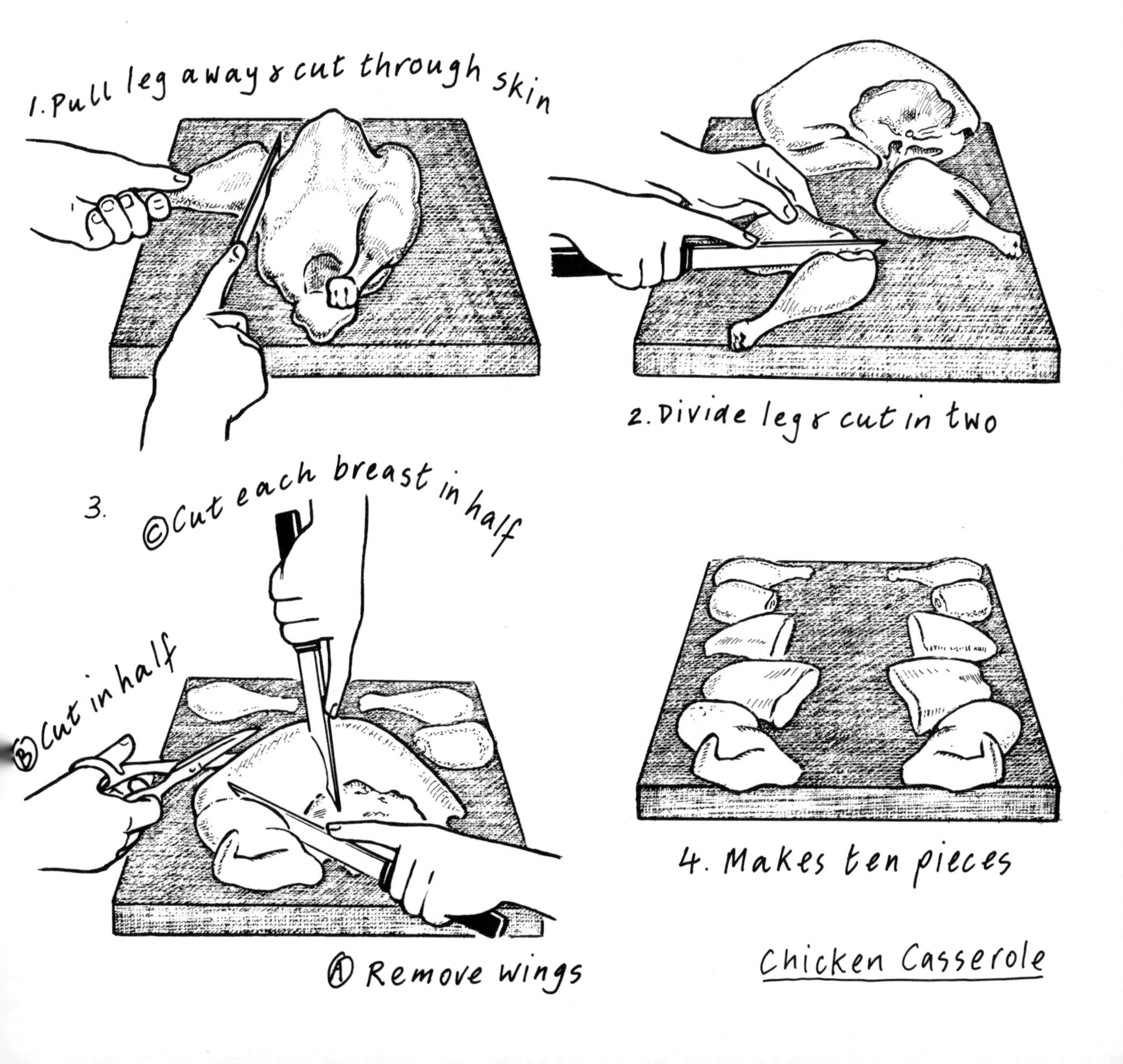


Chicken Casserole

CHAPTER SIX

# MAGIC/ TRANSFORMATIONS

---

GOLDEN HONEYCOMB · POPCORN

CANDIED CORN · TOFFEE APPLES

SPUN SUGAR · FRUIT KEBABS

FROSTED FRUIT · CANDIED FRUIT

BAKED ALASKA · INSTANT RASPBERRY SORBET

BRANDYSNAPS

Cooking is useful and creative and rewarding but it can also sometimes seem like magic. The laws of chemistry could be called upon to account for some of the transformations that take place in the kitchen, but often wizardry or alchemy seems the better explanation: sugar and water can be made to spin golden threads; kernels of corn explode into crisp clouds; bicarbonate of soda turns toffee into honeycomb; ice-cream can emerge from a hot oven sealed in by a snowy mountain tipped with gold; frozen fruit whirls into sorbet.

This chapter concentrates on just some, mostly sweet, usually quick, dramatic cooking ideas. They are recipes to round off a meal on a high note or fill deliciously an idle moment. But magic runs right through the book. Just think of soufflés rising, mayonnaise thickening, puris puffing . . .

## GOLDEN HONEYCOMB

This is great fun to make. The addition of bicarbonate of soda will make the mixture of butter, sugar and syrup foam and seethe like volcanic lava, and then the mixture sets firm into a substance resembling the inside of a Crunchie bar.

4 oz/110 g caster sugar
2 tbsp golden syrup
1 oz/30 g butter
1 tsp bicarbonate of soda
scrap of butter, for greasing the tin

Using kitchen paper or butter wrapping, wipe a small square cake tin, about 6 in/15 cm square, with a scrap of butter until it is lightly greased inside. Put the sugar, golden syrup (if you heat the spoon under the hot tap before dipping in, the syrup will slide off more easily) and butter into a medium-sized heavy-bottomed saucepan. Stir over a low heat until everything has melted and then continue to cook the mixture without stirring until it starts to turn a light brown. If it seems to be colouring unevenly, tip the pan rather than stir the mixture. When the mixture is a definite golden colour, remove from the heat and pour in the bicarbonate of soda. Stir immediately with a wooden spoon. The mixture will foam up and seethe in a very satisfying way. Pour it into the prepared tin. Let it cool and set and then break into pieces.

## POPCORN

Follow this method and your popcorn will be dry and fluffy, ready to absorb trickles of melted butter. Corn for popping has become quite easy to obtain in delicatessens and supermarkets. Health-food shops can usually be counted upon to sell it. Freshly popped corn is a whole different experience to corn bought already popped.

2 oz/55 g popping corn
enough vegetable oil just to cover the bottom of your chosen saucepan
salt
melted butter, to serve

Choose a saucepan that will hold the corn in a layer only one kernel deep. Cover the bottom with vegetable oil. Place it on the stove on a low heat, with just one kernel of corn in the pan. Wait for the one kernel to pop, remove it (it may well have jumped out) and add the rest of the corn. Continue to cook it on a low heat and when the corn starts to pop, cover the pan with a lid, turn the heat up to medium and, holding the pan with oven gloves or a thick cloth, shake it while the corn is popping. When it sounds like the whole battalion firing, turn up the heat a little and continue shaking the pan over the heat until the popping stops. Turn off the heat and uncover the pan, remembering that the odd kernel of corn can still surprise you by popping up. Add a few pinches of salt and shake around. Melt as much butter as you want and trickle it on.

## CANDIED CORN

If you like sweet popcorn, you can trickle sugar syrup over it and, if you wish, press the sticky popcorn into balls the size of your fist.

Make up the sugar syrup given in the recipe for Toffee Apples in this chapter. Cook as described until it is golden, and test to see if it is ready by dripping a drop into a cup of cold water. When ready, that drip will harden immediately. Pour the syrup over the popped corn. Stir the corn around with a long-handled wooden spoon until the syrup is well distributed. If you want to make popcorn balls,

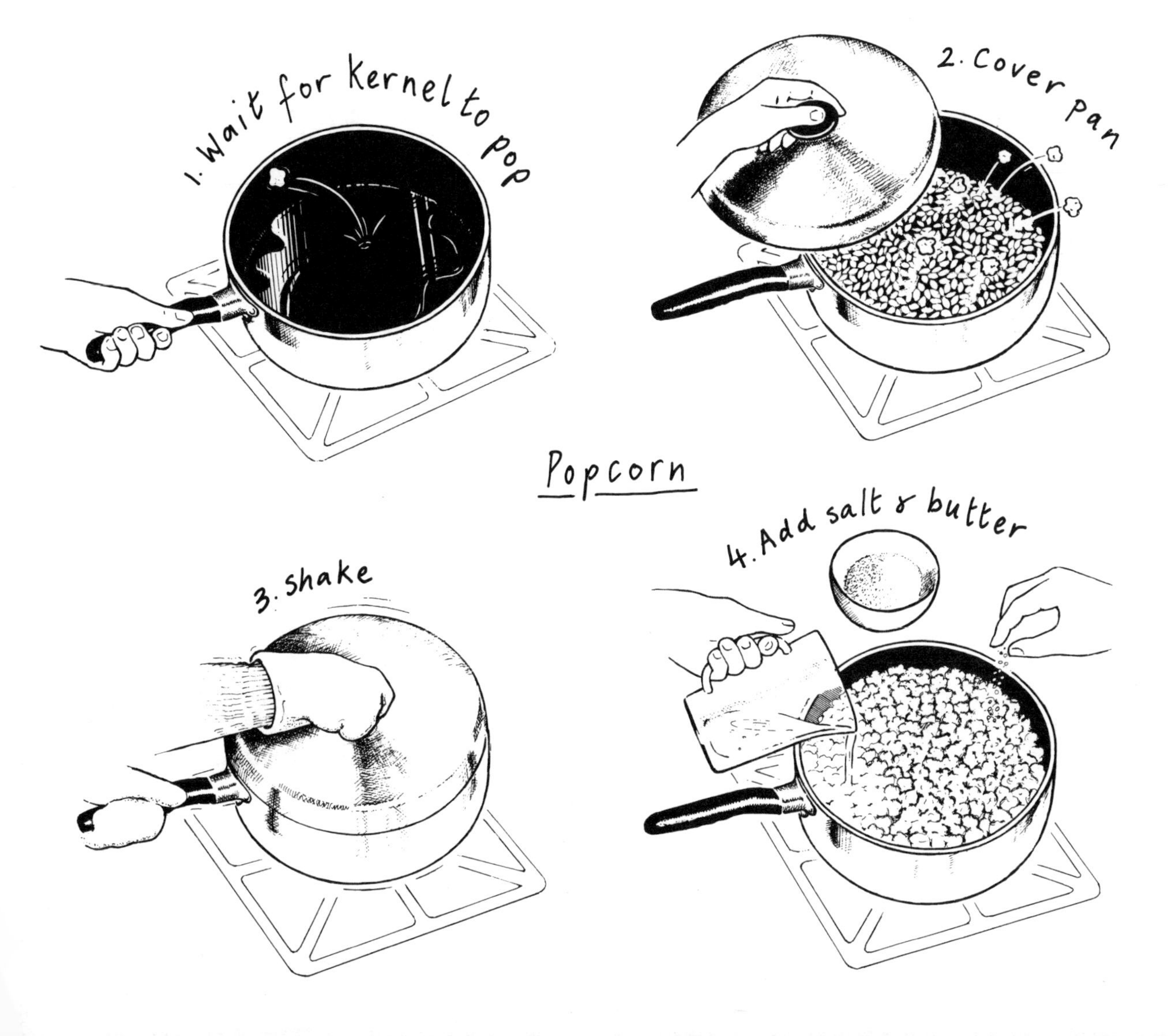

wait until the syrup has cooled, lightly oil your hands with vegetable oil and press the popcorn together into balls.

## TOFFEE APPLES

Hallowe'en, Guy Fawkes Day, any day, these are quick to make, nice to hand round.

4–6 hard dessert apples (Granny Smiths are ideal)
6 oz/170 g sugar
3 fl oz/85 ml water
1 tsp lemon juice
1 tsp vegetable oil, for oiling aluminium foil

Wash and dry the apples and remove any stalks. Push a wooden or cardboard stick (the sort sold for ice lollies) into each apple at the stalk end. Take a square of aluminium foil large enough to accommodate all the apples and oil it lightly by wiping the vegetable oil over it with a piece of kitchen paper.

Put the sugar and water into a medium-sized heavy-bottomed saucepan and melt the sugar over a low heat. Add the lemon juice and boil the mixture without stirring until it starts to colour. As it turns a light brown, take a fork and lift a bit of the mixture up. Wave the fork above the pan. The mixture should drop from the fork in a thread. If the colour in the pan is uneven, tip the pan around to spread it evenly. Remove the pan from the heat and twirl each apple in the caramel until it is covered. Stand the apples on the foil where a little pool of caramel will form around their bases and set hard. When hard all over on the outside, remove the apples from the foil and hand round.

## TO SPIN SUGAR

By 'pulling' boiled sugar, professional chefs can create amazing sculptures, pictures and edifices, but the simplest technique of making threads of toffee can decorate desserts very effectively. You might create a tangle of threads on top of fruit salad or stewed fruit or wind them round scoops of ice-cream or sorbet.

Make the caramel as described in the recipe for Toffee Apples. Use two forks to drip threads of the mixture on to desserts or around fruits. If you hold a fork up high, a long thread will spin down and you can weave it into a nest of golden twine by winding it round and round. By bringing the two forks together once they are coated on the ends with the caramel, and then pulling them apart, you can form several threads. Spinning sugar should be done soon before eating as after a while the threads will melt.

To clean the pan, which eventually will set hard with the caramel, soak it in warm water for an hour or two and the caramel will melt away.

## FRUIT KEBABS AND FROSTED FRUIT

Items of food threaded on to a stick are inviting and easy to eat. When fruit is served as kebabs everyone — even those who can't be bothered to peel a tangerine — wants some. Frosted fruit sparkles, crunches and dazzles either on its own or as part of the kebab.

An assortment of suitable fruit, e.g. grapes, cherries, raspberries, strawberries, pineapple, melon, mango, kiwi-fruit, star-fruit, papaya, apples, pears, tangerines, banana
1 lemon or 2 limes, for juice

**Frosting**
1 egg-white
granulated sugar

## FRUIT KEBABS

Cut or divide the fruit into bite-sized pieces. Squeeze lemon or lime juice over apples, pears and bananas to stop the fruit going brown (oxidizing) and over the other fruit if you like the tang of lemon. Using the thin wooden skewers sold for kebabs and satay, thread a mixture of fruit on to each one, allowing two skewers per person. Serve immediately or arrange on a plate, cover with clingfilm and refrigerate for an hour or two before serving.

## FROSTED FRUIT

Certain fruits can be frosted, which will provide prettiness and crunch. The best ones to use are those that are whole, such as grapes, cherries, strawberries and raspberries, and tangerine pieces with the skin intact so that they will not give off juice which would melt the frosting.

Prepare the fruit to be frosted, leaving stalks on the cherries and strawberries and as much stalk as possible on individual grapes or clusters of two or three grapes.

Separate the egg and put the white into a small, clean bowl. Keep the yolk in a cup covered with clingfilm for another use, perhaps to make mayonnaise (see p.52).

Using a fork, whip the egg-white, but only enough to break it up into a bubbly mass. Don't aim to make it white and foamy; you want to use it as glue. Pour a cupful of granulated sugar into a shallow bowl. Have a flat plate ready. Dip the fruits, bit by bit, into the egg-white and then into the sugar, rolling them around to get them evenly covered. Place on the plate. When you have finished, leave in a cool place (but not the refrigerator) for about an hour to let the coating set. Use them as an ingredient on the skewers or serve separately.

## CANDIED FRUIT

Instead of frosting fruit with grains of sugar, you can encase it in a shiny glassy layer of clear toffee. Follow the instructions for the sugar syrup in the recipe for Toffee Apples, cooking it to the stage where you coat the apples, and using tongs (not a fork which will pierce the skin of the fruit), twirl any of the fruits or segments of fruit suggested for frosted fruit in the syrup. Place them on a sheet of oiled foil and let them set. Eat within a few hours.

## BAKED ALASKA

Taking a dessert out of the oven that contains ice-cream at its centre would certainly seem to involve sleight of hand and will certainly amaze your friends! The secret behind making this flashy pudding is to have the oven very hot and the ice-cream very cold, and to use the meringue carefully to seal in the ice-cream. This foamy 'lagging' will puff up slightly and turn golden but insulate the cold heart of the matter.

Serves 4–5

1 home-made or bought flan (sponge cake) base
8 oz/225 g fresh soft fruit, e.g. strawberries, or stewed fruit, e.g. apricots
8 oz/225 g block of firmly frozen vanilla ice-cream
3 egg-whites
6 oz/170 g caster sugar

Put the sponge cake base on to an ovenproof dish that will fit into your freezer. Slice the block of ice-cream and arrange it to cover the sponge cake but leaving a margin of cake around the edge. Put the sponge and ice-cream into the freezer.

Turn on the oven to 450°F/230°C/gas mark 8.

Put the egg-whites into a clean, large bowl. Beat them with a hand rotary beater or hand-held electric beater until they form stiff, snowy peaks. Add 2 oz/55 g of the sugar and beat again until you have glistening peaks. Fold in the rest of the sugar with a metal spoon.

Take the sponge and ice-cream out of the freezer. Arrange your choice of fresh fruit on top of the ice-cream. Carefully spoon the meringue over the cake, making sure that it is well covered, leaving no gaps. Using a fork or knife, sculpt the meringue into swirls and peaks. Place in the hot oven for 3 to 4 minutes or until the meringue is lightly browned and the tips of the meringue a deep golden colour. Serve immediately.

## INSTANT RASPBERRY SORBET

You can now buy frozen soft fruit all the year round or, should you grow soft fruit such as raspberries, strawberries and currants, you may have some stored in your freezer. This method produces an instant sorbet tasting *intensely* of whatever fruit you choose.

Serves 4

12 oz/340 g packet frozen raspberries or strawberries
4 oz/110 g caster sugar
juice of half a small lemon

This recipe requires either a food processor or a liquidizer. The large bowl of the food processor is ideal. If you are using a liquidizer you will have to whizz the fruit in batches. Empty the frozen fruit into the bowl of the food processor equipped with its metal blade. Sprinkle the sugar on top and leave for 15 to 20 minutes until the sugar starts melting into the slightly softening fruit. Switch on the machine and either use the pulse button or, if there isn't one, switch on and off a few times until the fruit is just puréed and takes on the look of a sorbet. Add lemon juice to taste. Give one final whizz and either serve immediately or freeze the mixture until it is wanted.

## BRANDYSNAPS

A spell in the oven transforms beige blobs of uncooked brandysnaps into golden brown lacy mats that can be rolled up and will set into crisp, crackling tubes.

a generous 4 oz/125 g butter
4 oz/120 g caster sugar
4 oz/120 g golden syrup (see method)
4 oz/120 g plain flour
½ tsp ground ginger

Turn on the oven to 375°F/190°C/gas mark 5.

Weigh the butter and put into the top half of a double boiler. Weigh the sugar, then add the golden syrup on top of the sugar on the scales until the weight of 8 oz/240 g is reached. Tip the sugar and syrup into the pan to join the butter. This method gets around the problem of stickiness in measuring golden syrup. Stir these ingredients over simmering water until they are melted and blended. Remove from the heat and stir in the flour gradually. Add ginger and stir again. Lightly oil two baking sheets, using a few drops of vegetable oil and some kitchen paper. Spoon four or five rounds of the mixture on to one of the baking sheets, leaving large spaces in between. Put them in the oven. Five minutes later, load the second baking sheet and put that in the oven. Five minutes later, check the first batch and if the mixture has spread and coloured a deep and bubbling brown, remove from the oven. Here is the mildly tricky part. Wait a few minutes until the biscuits begin to solidify but still remain bendy. Remove them one at a time from the tin with a spatula or fish slice and roll them loosely round the handles of wooden spoons. As they cool they will become hard and crisp and can be slid off on to a wire tray. Continue in this way, alternating the baking sheets until all the mixture is cooked.

Note: If you leave the biscuits too long on the trays and they become too brittle to handle, soften them by putting them back in the oven for a minute.

CHAPTER SEVEN

# VEGETARIAN FOOD

CRUDITÉS WITH DIPS · GUACAMOLE

BLUE CHEESE DIP · CURRY DIP

THOUSAND ISLAND DRESSING · SATAY SAUCE

HUMMUS · FRIED AUBERGINE

LEEK AND POTATO SOUP · BAKED POTATOES

TOMATO SAUCE · PESTO · MUSHROOM SAUCE

FRIED EGG WITH CHILLIS OR GARLIC

STIR-FRIED VEGETABLES · FRIED BEANCURD

PIZZA · TUNA SALAD · GREEN SALAD

CAESAR SALAD ALMOST · GARLIC BREAD

This chapter on vegetarian food is included separately not in order to suggest that vegetarians are a race apart — there are many recipes in the rest of the book that will please — but to give some additional ideas. All too often those who choose to forgo meat are landed with just an omelette or a dreary assembly of lettuce leaves, tomatoes, spring onions and grated cheese, called Cheese Salad. More and more people are taking the vegetarian way, and it is important that any diet should not be repetitive or, as is a risk with meatless meals, stodgy. Inspiration and ideas from oriental and Middle-Eastern cuisines are a great help here. The assumption in this chapter is that dairy foods and fish are allowable, but the recipes that would also please a vegan are marked with an asterisk (*).

## CRUDITÉS WITH A SELECTION OF DIPS

The word *crudités* is just a useful borrowing from French, meaning a selection of raw vegetables. For anyone wishing to eat in a healthy manner or trying to lose weight, having a selection of crudités prepared and crisping in the refrigerator is a great help. More vegetables than you might imagine are good eaten raw. A lot of the appeal lies in the preparation.

All these vegetables can be scrubbed or peeled and cut into long slender strips: carrots, celery, courgettes, green, yellow and red peppers, spring onions, fennel, endive and cucumber.

The following can be sliced or broken off into small, manageable pieces or podded:

Crudités & Dips

mushrooms wiped clean, cauliflower, broccoli, young broad beans, fresh peas, tomatoes, radishes and watercress.

Arrange your choice of vegetables (the above is only a guideline) on a bed of ice in a bowl. Eat with any of the following dips:

## GARLIC MAYONNAISE (AIOLI)

See recipe in Chapter Four (p.000)

## * AVOCADO SAUCE (GUACAMOLE)

1 very ripe avocado
1 clove of garlic
1 tomato (optional)
1 dsp lemon juice
1 tsp chilli sauce
1 tbsp olive oil or vegetable oil
salt and pepper

Peel the clove of garlic and chop it finely or squeeze it through a garlic press. If you want to use a tomato, skin it by putting it into a bowl, covering it with boiling water and leaving it for a minute. Spear the tomato on a fork and remove it from the water. The skin will now slip off easily. Chop the tomato finely and let any watery juice run away. Cut the avocado in half and remove the stone. Scoop out the flesh from the skins and put into a shallow dish. Mash with a fork into a lumpy cream. Stir in the chopped or crushed garlic, the tomato pieces, the lemon juice, chilli sauce, oil and a pinch of salt and pepper. When it is all well mixed, taste and see if you want to increase the spiciness.

Note: Guacamole served with Mexican tortilla chips (tostadas) or other savoury crackers makes a very good course on its own.

## BLUE CHEESE DIP

1 carton soured cream
2 oz/60 g blue cheese — left-over cheese is ideal for this
dash of Tabasco or Worcestershire sauce

Chop finely or crumble the cheese. Stir it into the soured cream and add a dash of one of the sauces.

Note: Soured cream with its slightly sharp taste and thick texture is an ideal base for dips; a handful of chopped fresh herbs stirred into the cream is simple and excellent. A favourite American dip is soured cream into which you stir the contents of a packet of dried onion soup mix.

## CURRY DIP

The important thing about flavouring a dip with curry powder is gently cooking the curry powder to remove its 'raw' taste. In 1 oz/30 g of butter or vegetable oil, slowly cook 1 teaspoonful of curry powder for 2 minutes. Let the mixture cool and then stir it into a carton of soured cream or a cup of mayonnaise.

## THOUSAND ISLAND DRESSING

There seems no agreement on what is the authentic Thousand Island Dressing, so feel free to vary the recipe below.

4 tbsp mayonnaise
1 tbsp tomato ketchup
1 tbsp chopped sweet pickle or chopped up dill pickles
chilli sauce, to taste
1 tbsp chopped fresh herbs such as chives and/or parsley if available
1 egg, hard-boiled and finely chopped (optional)
salt and pepper
pinch of sugar

Mix the ingredients together. Taste for seasoning and adjust to suit yourself.

## * SATAY SAUCE

This peanut-based sauce is usually served as an accompaniment to skewers of grilled meat but is also good as a dip for vegetables — which could also be grilled on skewers when life in the raw gets too much for you.

1 onion, peeled and finely chopped
1 tbsp vegetable oil
6 oz/170 g crunchy peanut butter
1 tsp sugar
juice of half a lemon
finely chopped chillis or chilli sauce to taste
1 tbsp soy sauce

Fry the chopped onion in the oil until it is golden. Add half a teaspoon of chilli sauce or a few strands of fresh chilli (or omit the chilli altogether if you dislike 'hot' food). Stir in the peanut butter, about 6 fl oz/175 ml of water and the sugar. Stir and simmer until you have a fairly thick mixture. Add lemon juice and soy sauce and stir again. Use when warm or cool.

## * HUMMUS

This Middle-Eastern dip or first course (serve with hot pitta bread) can be made from dried or tinned chick peas. If using dried chick peas, you have to plan ahead as they must be soaked overnight. Chick peas are one of the few items that seem to come to no harm, in terms of flavour and texture, by being tinned. Tahina or sesame seed paste can be bought in most enterprising supermarkets and in oriental grocery stores.

1 x 15 oz/435 g tin of chick peas *or* 4–6 oz/110–170 g dried chick peas, soaked overnight in cold water
juice of a lemon
2 tbsp tahina (sesame seed paste)
2 cloves of garlic
salt

*Garnish*
1 tbsp olive oil
1 tsp cayenne pepper or paprika
1 tsp ground cumin (optional)

Open the tin of chick peas and drain them. If you are cooking the chick peas, drain them from their soaking water, put them in a pan well covered with fresh water and simmer for an hour or so until they are tender. The length of time they take will depend on the age of the chick peas but it is hard to overcook them. When they are cooked, drain them, keeping some of the water.

Put the chick peas in the bowl of a food processor with 1 tablespoonful of lemon juice, 2 tablespoonfuls of the cooking water or fresh water, the tahina and the garlic which you have peeled and crushed. Whizz to a rough puree — you want knobbly, knubbly bits to contribute to the texture. Taste and see if you want to add more lemon juice. This will thin the mixture a bit more which you might also want to do. If you want a thinner mixture without more lemony flavour, use water. Add salt to taste. Scoop out the hummus into a serving dish. Mix the oil with the cayenne or paprika and dribble it on in a pretty pattern. To complete a Persian carpet effect, make lines or streaks with ground cumin.

If you do not have a food processor, you can use a liquidizer, but in this case make the hummus in batches. You could also pound the chick peas in a pestle and mortar, but this is quite hard labour.

## * FRIED AUBERGINE

These crisp slices go well with a dip of garlic mayonnaise or a dollop of plain yoghurt or as a side order with the hummus.

1 medium-sized aubergine
1 oz/30 g plain flour
salt and pepper
vegetable oil or olive oil, for frying

Trim both ends off the aubergine and then slice it into pieces about ¼in/0.5 cm thick. Lay these on a plate and sprinkle lightly with salt. Turn them over and sprinkle the other sides. Leave for about 20 minutes, after which time the slices will have 'sweated' out some liquid. Dab the beads of sweat away with kitchen paper. This removes any bitter taste and stops the aubergine slices absorbing too much oil. On another clean large plate scatter the flour and season it with salt and pepper. Turn the slices in the flour, shaking off any excess so that they are just lightly dusted. Heat up oil in a frying pan to a depth of about ½ in/1 cm. With the corner of an aubergine slice, test the oil to see if it is hot enough and sizzles when it comes in contact with the aubergine. If so, fry the slices, three or four at a time, turning once, until they are golden. Drain on kitchen paper and keep them warm while cooking the rest. Serve immediately.

## * LEEK AND POTATO SOUP (VICHYSSOISE)

This classic soup is easy to make and once you understand the process — 'sweating' the vegetables, adding stock, simmering until tender, then sieving or liquidizing and enriching with cream and seasonings — you can adapt it to use other vegetables. Carrots added to the recipe below give you the favourite soup of the French kitchen, *Potage Bonne Femme* or Good Woman's Soup.

Serves 4

1 onion
4 leeks
2 medium-sized potatoes
1½ oz/45 g butter
1½ pints/860 ml stock (use a vegetarian stock cube or, if you have none, water will do)
1 tbsp cream (optional)
salt and pepper
1 tbsp chopped parsley or chives

Peel the onion and chop it into small pieces. Trim the root end of the leeks, cut off the leaves leaving only a very little dark green and cut a slit right through the top part of the leeks to help in flushing out any grit or sand. Wash them thoroughly. Slice into rings about ¼ in/0.5 cm wide. Peel the potatoes and chop them into quite small pieces. Melt the butter in a medium to large saucepan and cook the leeks and onion over a low heat until they are softened. Add the potatoes and turn them over and over until they glisten with butter. Pour in the stock and simmer for 20 to 30 minutes or until the potatoes are tender. Take the soup off the heat, let it cool a little and then liquidize or blend in a food processor. Return the soup to the pan and check the consistency. You may want to thin it with a little milk or more stock. Season with salt and pepper, add the parsley or chives and the cream if you are using it. Let the soup simmer for a few minutes and then serve. This soup is also very good chilled in the refrigerator and served cold.

## * BAKED POTATOES

Baked potatoes are particularly nutritious if you eat the skins, which contain an invigorating amount of vitamin D. When rubbed with oil and salt before baking, the skins will glisten, crackle and beg to be eaten.

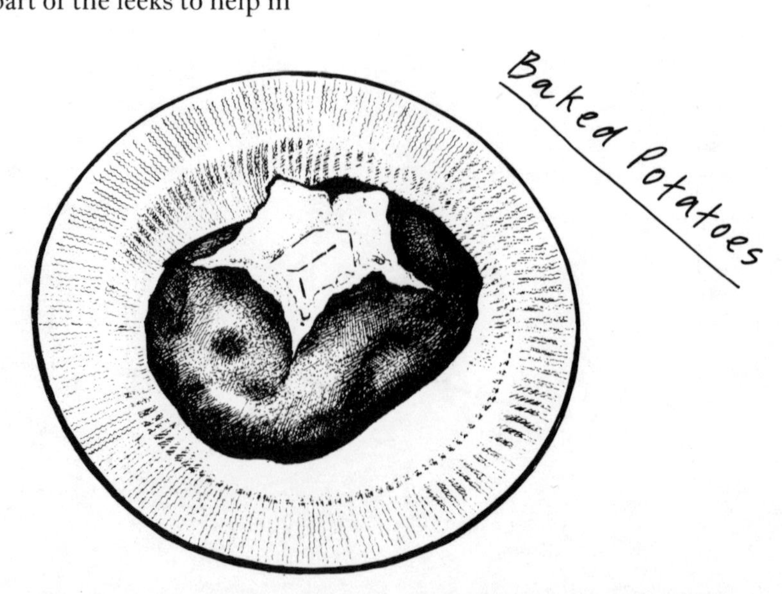

1–2 potatoes per person (large potatoes bake best and Lincolnshire Whites bake best of all)
vegetable oil
salt, preferably sea salt

Turn on the oven to 400°F/200°C/gas mark 6.

Wash the potatoes, dry them and rub them all over with a little vegetable oil. Sprinkle them with salt and put in the oven for 1 hour or, if you are using small potatoes, for 45 minutes. Using stout oven gloves, remove them from the oven. With a sharp knife cut a cross in the top of each potato to a depth of about 1 in/2 cm. Using oven gloves, squeeze the sides of the potato to open up the cross. Serve with a generous pat of butter or the filling of your choice or one selected from the following:

soured cream and chopped chives or parsley
grated Cheddar cheese
a slice of Boursin cheese
baked beans, heated up

## PASTA SAUCES

Dried pasta in all its varieties, as well as the fresh pasta now readily available, is a great standby for vegetarians. It can be cooked quickly and dressed simply with butter and grated cheese (preferably Parmesan) or with oil in which you have heated some slivers of garlic, or there is a wide variety of vegetarian sauces for a more elaborate meal. Some ideas are given below.

Cook pasta in plenty of boiling water into which you put a generous pinch of salt and a dessertspoonful of oil, which helps stop the pasta sticking. Allow 3 to 4 oz/85 to 110 g pasta per person. Follow the timing instructions on the packet but start testing to see if it is done quite a few minutes before it is due to be ready, as it is important not to overcook pasta. Using a fork, fish out a strand, let the hot water drain off and bite it. When the pasta is ready it will be tender but with just a little resistance to the teeth, what the Italians call *al dente*. Drain it in a colander or large sieve, return it to the pan or put it in a warmed serving dish, and toss with your chosen sauce. Pasta cools quickly so it is important to serve it on warmed plates or in warm bowls.

## * TOMATO SAUCE

2 tbsp oil (preferably olive oil)
1 medium-sized onion
2 cloves of garlic
1 x 15 oz/435 g tin peeled or peeled and chopped tomatoes
salt and pepper
pinch of sugar
some fresh basil leaves if available or substitute ½ tsp dried oregano

Peel and chop the onion finely. Peel the cloves of garlic and crush or sliver them. (You can leave out the garlic but it would be a pity.) Heat the oil in a medium-sized pan or frying pan and gently cook the onion and garlic. When the onion is softened and beginning to look golden, tip in the tomatoes and stir them around with a wooden spoon, breaking them up if they are whole. Cook for about 5 minutes, stirring, until some of the liquid has evaporated and the sauce looks thick. Flavour with salt, pepper and a pinch of sugar and the oregano if you are using it. Cook for a few more minutes. If you are able to get fresh basil, tear up about 5 or 6 leaves and add them now. Basil and tomato are beautifully complementary flavours. Serve on spaghetti or any shape of pasta and serve hand-grated cheese separately.

## * COLD TOMATO SAUCE

The combination of hot pasta and cold tomato sauce is wonderful — light and healthy, almost like a salad.

3 large or 4 medium-sized tomatoes
4 spring onions
2 tbsp vegetable oil (preferably olive oil)
1 tbsp wine vinegar
salt and pepper
pinch of sugar
1 tbsp chopped parsley
a few basil leaves if possible

With a sharp knife cut a cross in each tomato at the stalk end. Put the tomatoes in a bowl. Bring a large kettleful of water to the boil and when it is boiling, carefully pour enough water on to the tomatoes to cover them. Leave them for a minute and then drain the water off. You can now easily peel the skins off the tomatoes. Chop the tomatoes finely, discarding the hard bits round the stalk end and the watery juices. Put the chopped tomatoes into a shallow bowl. Peel the spring onions. Trim them at both ends, leaving about 2 in/5 cm of the dark green leaves. Chop the onions into slender rings. Add to the tomatoes. Add oil, vinegar, salt, pepper, sugar and parsley and torn-up basil leaves if you have them and stir around. Leave for about 5 minutes (or longer) for the flavours to mix. When the pasta is ready, drained and hot, add the cold sauce, mix quickly and serve immediately.

## * PESTO

Pesto is a sauce made from basil, pine kernels, garlic, Parmesan cheese and olive oil but, if you do not want to make it from scratch, there is a perfectly good bottled version generally available in delicatessens and supermarkets. To dress enough pasta for four people, gently heat 2 to 3 tablespoonfuls of the bottled sauce with 1 tablespoonful of vegetable oil, stirring until you have a smooth mixture. Pour on to the hot cooked pasta and toss like a salad.

## MUSHROOM SAUCE

2 oz/55 g butter or 2 tbsp vegetable oil
8 oz/225 g mushrooms
1 clove of garlic
5 oz/140 g cream or Greek (thick) yoghurt or low-fat white cheese
salt and pepper

Wipe the mushrooms clean with a damp cloth or damp kitchen paper. Trim the ends of the stalks and slice into thin slices. Peel the garlic clove and chop finely. Melt the butter or heat up the oil and gently fry the mushrooms and garlic for a few minutes or until the mushrooms are soft and giving off juice. Add the cream or yoghurt or soft cheese and stir until well mixed. Season with a pinch of salt and a generous amount of pepper. Pour on to hot pasta and mix.

## FRIED EGG WITH CHILLIS OR GARLIC

A fried egg on top of a small bowl of spaghetti makes a quick and delicious meal, the yolk of the egg becoming the sauce. The chilli or garlic heated up in the oil gives it a nice bite.

1 egg per person
1 tbsp oil (preferably olive oil)
2 dried chillis *or* 1 fat clove of garlic
salt and pepper

Heat up the oil in a small frying pan. Peel and slice the garlic or break each chilli in two. Fry the garlic or chillis gently for 2 to 3 minutes. Using a slotted spoon, remove the garlic or chillis. Break the egg into the pan and cook gently until the white is set. Season with salt and pepper. Place the egg on top of the pasta and pour the hot flavoured oil over. Let each person break the yolk of the egg and allow it to run over the pasta.

## STIR-FRIED VEGETABLES

Thinly cut stir-fried vegetables (follow the recipe below) are good mixed into pasta and when served like this make a complete meal. When choosing the vegetables, keep in mind that broccoli goes particularly well with pasta.

## * STIR-FRIED VEGETABLES AND BEANCURD

For stir-frying vegetables a wok is the ideal pan, but you can use a large frying pan. The advantage of a wok is its bowl shape which means you can use less oil and there is a larger surface for cooking the vegetables. Vegetables can be stir-fried individually or as a mixture. If they are cut thinly they will cook with a minimum of liquid. Sometimes a splash of soy sauce at the end is enough. Slivers of fresh root ginger are a good addition to stir-fried vegetables and root ginger is now stocked by most supermarkets and many greengrocers and by all oriental stores. The recipe below is only a guideline. Most vegetables can be stir-fried, so let your taste and what is on hand dictate your choice.

# Stir-Fried Vegetables

Serves 4

2–3 tbsp vegetable oil
3 stalks celery
2 large carrots
1 bunch spring onions
2 oz/55 g mange-tout peas
2 oz/55 g broccoli
2 oz/55 g beansprouts
1-in/2-cm piece of ginger root (optional)
1 fat clove of garlic (optional)
1 dsp soy sauce

Prepare the vegetables. Clean the celery and take off any obvious strings. Cut it on the diagonal into pieces about ¼ in/0.5 cm thick. Peel the carrots and slice them, also on the diagonal, into thin pieces. Take the outer skin off the spring onion and trim at both ends, leaving about 2 in/5 cm of the dark green leaves on. Chop into thin rings. Top and tail the mange-tout peas. Trim the stalks of the broccoli. Cut the hard stalk into thin rings and the heads into small bunches. Rinse the beansprouts only if you think they need it. Drain them thoroughly. Peel the ginger root and either cut into thin matchsticks or take off paper-thin slices using a vegetable slicer. Peel the garlic clove and cut into tiny chips.

Pour the oil into the wok or frying pan (you will need the larger quantity of oil in the frying pan). When it is hot, add the garlic and ginger and sizzle for 30 seconds. Add the celery, carrots, spring onions, mange-tout peas and broccoli and stir around in the hot oil, swirling the oil around the wok and flipping the vegetables over with a wok spoon or fish slice. Keep stirring until the vegetables are just tender — about 3 to 4 minutes. If they start to stick and burn, add 1 tablespoonful of water. You want to keep them a little bit crisp. Add the soy sauce. Give a final swirl and serve on noodles or with rice or with cubes of fried beancurd (see below).

## * FRIED BEANCURD

Beancurd, a bland, cushiony substance made from a mixture of finely ground soy beans and water, available from oriental grocers and health-food shops, is an important source of protein for vegetarians and an ideal accompaniment to stir-fried vegetables. Beancurd is sold in blocks. It can be cut into cubes and deep-fried or floured and fried as described here. Wholemeal flour lends a nutty taste.

1 block beancurd
1 oz/30 g wholemeal flour
salt and pepper
2 tbsp vegetable oil, for frying

Cut the block of beancurd into 8 squares. Let them sit on kitchen paper to drain. Sprinkle the flour on a plate and season with salt and pepper. Heat the oil in a frying pan. Roll the cubes of the beancurd in the seasoned flour and fry, turning carefully with a spatula, until they are browned and have a crisp outside skin. Remove the beancurd cubes and serve on top of stir-fried vegetables.

## PIZZA

Using the basic dough recipe in Chapter Three you can make a perfect pizza base, but for instant pizzas you can also use baps sliced in half horizontally or French bread cut in half lengthwise. Toppings for pizza can be varied according to taste and the recipe below is a basic one to which you can add 'side orders' such as anchovies, olives, mushrooms etc. It is worth buying mozzarella cheese, even the Danish kind, for the particular gummy way it melts.

Serves 4–6

8 oz/225 g bread dough, made according to the basic recipe in Chapter Three (p.32)
2 tbsp vegetable oil or olive oil
1 large clove of garlic
1 x 15 oz/435 g tin of peeled or peeled and chopped tomatoes
1 tbsp tomato purée or paste
salt and pepper
pinch of sugar
1 tsp dried oregano or basil
3 oz/85 g mozzarella or Bel Paese cheese
extra oil
additional ingredients to taste, e.g. anchovies, olives, mushrooms

Pizza

Make the dough following the instructions up to the knock-down stage. Roll out the dough into two circles and place on greased baking sheets or in large flan tins. Pinch up the edges of the circles of dough which will help keep the filling inside. Let them 'prove' while you make the filling. Peel the garlic and chop it finely. Heat up the oil and add the garlic and a minute later the tomatoes and tomato purée or paste. Cook, stirring from time to time, until you have quite a thick mixture. Season with salt, pepper and sugar. Take off the heat and let cool a little.

Turn on the oven to 400°F/230°C/gas mark 8.

Divide the tomato filling between the two pizzas. Sprinkle on the oregano or basil. Cut the cheese into thin slices and lay on top. Add any extra ingredients you fancy. Trickle on a little extra oil and bake in the hot oven for 20 minutes. Serve in sections while hot or warm.

## TUNA SALAD

If you eat fish, tinned tuna fish is a handy item to have in the store cupboard. Mixed with mayonnaise, celery and spring onion it makes a main-course salad or an excellent sandwich filling, especially with wholemeal toast.

1 x 7 oz/200 g tin of tuna fish packed in either oil or brine
2 heaped tbsp mayonnaise, either home-made (see Chapter Four, p.000) or bought
4 spring onions
2 stalks celery
salt and pepper
lettuce leaves, for cradling the salad or layering in the sandwich

Open the tin of tuna and drain away the oil or brine. Peel the outer layer from the spring onions and trim them at each end, leaving about 2 in / 5 cm of dark green leaves. Chop them finely. Clean and de-string the celery. Cut in half lengthwise and then chop finely. Mix the spring onions, celery and mayonnaise into the tuna using a fork. Keep going until you have a creamy mixture. Season with salt and pepper. Serve either as a salad or as a sandwich filling.

## * GREEN SALAD DRESSED WITH VINAIGRETTE

The goodness of a green salad is dependent on its dressing. The simplest salad, just a bowl of lettuce leaves, can be a great treat when the dressing is right and for the most part this means balancing the relationship of oil to vinegar. Leave more elaborate dressings (for example the Thousand Island or the Blue Cheese in the Crudités recipe) for salads such as celery, apple and walnut or shredded cabbage with grated carrot (coleslaw). Green salad can contain a mixture of different varieties of lettuce together with items such as watercress, cucumber, celery, spring onion, green pepper, parsley and chives; the choice is up to you.

a mixture of salad vegetables (see above)
1 tbsp wine vinegar
½ tsp salt
half a clove of garlic (optional)
½ tsp black pepper
3 tbsp vegetable oil, preferably olive oil or a mixture of olive oil and vegetable oil

Measure the vinegar into a small bowl. Add the salt and pepper and the chopped or crushed garlic if you are using it. If you are dubious about garlic or want just the flavour to creep up on you, use the half-clove to rub the inside of the salad bowl. Stir the vinegar and flavourings with a metal spoon until the salt dissolves. Add the oil and blend it in using the back of the spoon. Toss the salad with the dressing just before eating, because if you do it too long in advance the acidity of the vinegar will wilt the leaves.

## CAESAR SALAD ALMOST

The following recipe does not give the correct way to make Caesar salad, a dish invented by a restaurateur in Tijuana in Mexico. That is better done by a waiter standing at a trolley in a restaurant. What this method does point up is the use of *croûtons* to make a salad more crunchy and substantial. Thickening the vinaigrette with an egg-yolk is a technique you can also use when dressing other salads.

lettuce leaves (iceberg, cos or Dutch lettuce or a mixture)
2 slices bread, brown or white
2 tbsp vegetable oil
vinaigrette as above
1 egg-yolk
1 tsp Worcestershire sauce
1 tbsp finely grated cheese, preferably Parmesan but any hard cheese will do

Wash the lettuce leaves if they need it and dry them carefully in a clean tea-towel or a salad-shaker or one of those plastic spin-driers. Place in a salad bowl. Cut the slices of bread into cubes of about ½ in / 1 cm. Heat up the oil and fry the bread cubes, turning them with a spatula until they are golden brown and crisp all over. Remove them from the pan and let them drain on kitchen paper. Make up the vinaigrette, stirring in the egg-yolk to thicken it and make it more silky. Put the fried bread cubes (*croûtons*) on to the lettuce leaves. Pour on the dressing. Sprinkle over the Worcestershire sauce and the grated cheese and toss the salad thoroughly until all the lettuce leaves are coated with dressing.

## GARLIC BREAD

Everybody loves this and it fills out a meal and makes it special.

1 long French bread (*baguette*)
3–4 oz/85–110 g butter, allowed to become soft at room temperature
2–3 cloves of garlic (depending on how strong you like it and how fat the cloves are)
1 tbsp finely chopped fresh parsley (optional)

Turn on the oven to 400°F/200°C/gas mark 6.

(Try to make this when the oven is already being used for another dish.)

With a sharp knife slice the bread at 1-in / 2-cm intervals, cutting down to the bottom but not through the bottom. Mix the butter with the peeled and chopped or crushed garlic and the parsley if you are using it. Spread the butter between the slices. If there is any butter left, spread it along the length of the top of the bread. Wrap the loaf in aluminium foil and bake in the oven for 30 minutes.

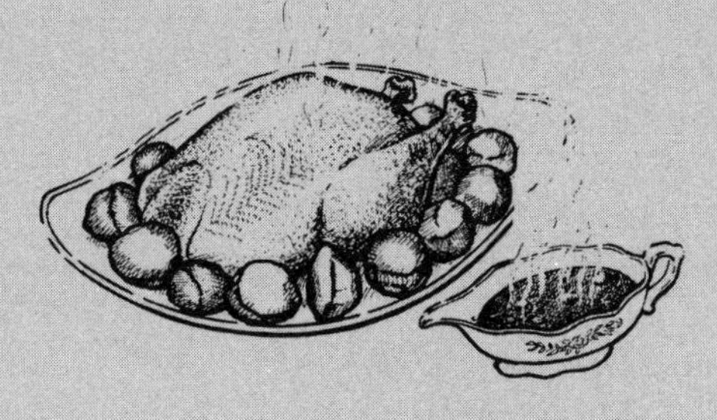

CHAPTER EIGHT

# A COMPLETE MEAL

PRAWN COCKTAIL · AVOCADO VINAIGRETTE

ROAST CHICKEN · ROAST BEEF

ROAST LAMB · ROAST POTATOES · CRUMBLES

BUTTERSCOTCH SAUCE

Once you are interested in cooking, the moment comes when you want to make a complete meal for family or friends. Any problem encountered is more likely to be with timing than with cooking. If you intend to serve three courses, getting everything ready at the appropriate moment is a job that sometimes seems to need the skills of the operations room of an army at the front line. It is important not to be over-ambitious. Choose at least one and maybe two courses that can be prepared ahead of time and need no last-minute attention. Concentrate your time and motion abilities on orchestrating the main course so that the meat or fish is ready at the same moment as the accompanying vegetables. Alternatively decide on a dish such as Spaghetti Bolognese (see Chapter Five, p.60) that needs only a Green Salad (see Chapter Seven, p.88) to go with it. Nowadays two courses with perhaps some cheese is often all that people want, and it is better to be able to relax and enjoy yourself than to overload your guests with food that they might feel duty bound to eat.

Since Sunday lunch is a time when you might feel like preparing a serious meal rather than one dish or a snack, in this chapter there are guidelines for roasting meat and instructions for roasting potatoes. Roast chicken, which is popular with almost everybody, is a good dish to try first. The transformation of a pallid bird into something proud, golden, juicy and aromatic is extremely satisfying to cook and customers alike. Of course, a casserole needs less precise timing and a dish such as Goulash (see Chapter Five, p.64) served with Dumplings (see Chapter Three, p.35) makes a wonderfully welcoming winter meal, as does an Irish stew.

For first courses and desserts there are some suggestions of recipes given in other chapters in the book as well as some additional ideas. Remember when deciding on your meal to balance the weight of the dishes. If you are having a substantial main course, such as roast beef with Yorkshire pudding, then it makes sense to start with something light, such as guacamole or Caesar salad, and finish with something refreshing, such as fruit kebabs.

## FIRST COURSES

### PRAWN COCKTAIL

Serves 4

8 oz/225 peeled prawns, preferably fresh but frozen will do
4 tbsp mayonnaise, either home-made (see Chapter Four, p.52) or bought
1 tbsp tomato ketchup
1 tbsp double cream or plain yoghurt
2 tsp lemon juice
dash of Worcestershire sauce
salt and pepper
1 lettuce
½ tsp paprika or cayenne pepper

If you are using frozen prawns, defrost them slowly — in the refrigerator is best. Drain them and pile them on to kitchen paper to dry some more. Cut the stalk end off the lettuce. Select

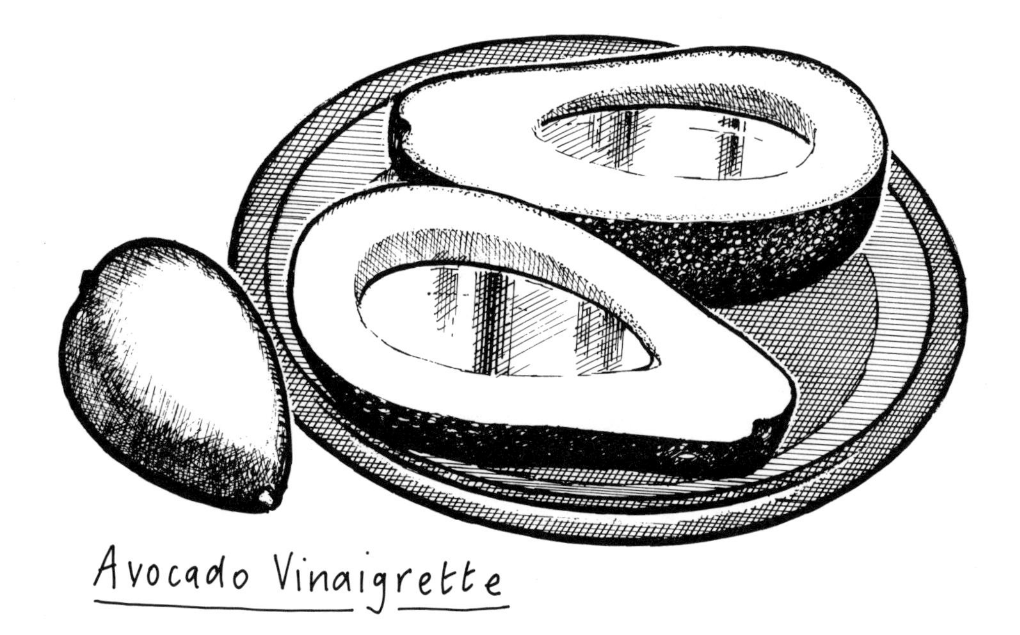


the best leaves. Put them in a pile and with a sharp knife cut them into narrow strips no more than ¼ in/0.5 cm wide. Fill four wide-mouthed wine glasses with the lettuce strips. Mix together the mayonnaise, ketchup, cream or yoghurt, lemon juice and Worcestershire sauce. Season with salt and pepper. Taste to check whether you need more of any of the flavours. Divide the prawns between the four glasses and then pour equal amounts of sauce on to each. Sprinkle with cayenne pepper or paprika.

## AVOCADO VINAIGRETTE

Serves 4

2 ripe avocados — ripe avocados are soft to the touch
1 tbsp wine vinegar
3 tbsp vegetable oil
salt and pepper
dry English mustard

Mix the wine vinegar with a pinch of salt, pepper and dry English mustard in a small bowl or jug. When the salt seems to have dissolved, stir in the oil. Taste to see if you need more of any seasoning. Just before serving them, cut the avocados in half by using a sharp knife to work your way round the longest route. Pull them apart — they come apart very easily. Remove the stones. Place each avocado half, skin side down, on a small plate and fill the hollow where the stone was with some vinaigrette.

Note: The prawns mixed into their cocktail sauce can also be used to fill the avocados.

**Ideas from Other Chapters**

Baked Eggs — p.48
Guacamole — p.79
Hummus with Pitta Bread — p.80
Leek and Potato Soup (Vichyssoise), hot or cold — p.82
Caesar Salad Almost — p.89

## MAIN COURSES

## ROAST CHICKEN

1 x 3–4 lb/1.35–1.8 kg roasting chicken
2 oz/55 g butter or 2 tbsp vegetable oil
2 cloves of garlic (optional)
half a lemon
salt and pepper
1 tsp mixed herbs or oregano

*Gravy*
2 tsp flour
½ pint/290 ml chicken stock or water from cooking vegetables

Turn on the oven to 400°F/200°C/gas mark 6.

Put half of the butter or oil inside the chicken and season the inside of the chicken with salt and pepper. If you are going to use garlic, crush the cloves with the back of a knife and put them inside the chicken as well. Spread the rest of the butter or oil over the breast and thighs of the chicken. Season with salt and pepper. Squeeze the juice of the lemon half over the chicken and put the squeezed half inside it. Place the prepared bird into a roasting pan and put it in the oven. After 15 minutes, using stout oven gloves remove the pan from the oven and spoon the butter or oil over the top of the chicken. This is called basting. Baste twice more at 15-minute intervals. If the chicken is browning too deeply, cover the breast with aluminium foil. The chicken will be cooked after 1 hour. Test to see whether it is done by piercing the plump part of thigh with a small sharp knife. The juices should run clear, not pink.

Remove the chicken to a warm serving plate and keep warm in the turned-off oven while you make the gravy. Place the roasting pan on the stove on a medium heat. Using a wooden spoon, stir in the flour and scrape up all the crusty bits that are sticking to the pan. When the flour is light brown, gradually add the stock, stirring all the while. Let it bubble and thicken, and season if necessary with a little salt and pepper. Strain into a warm gravy boat.

## ROAST BEEF

It is not worth roasting a very small piece of beef as the result will be tough. If you are lucky enough to have a piece of rib or sirloin weighing 4 lb/1.8 kg or more, then you can roast it, allowing 20 minutes per 1 lb/450 g for medium-rare meat. Turn on the oven to 425°F/220°C/gas mark 7. Place the beef in a roasting tin or on a rack in a roasting tin. Spread with a little butter, oil or dripping and sprinkle on some dry English mustard and black pepper. Do not add salt at this point as it will draw out the juices of the meat. Roast at this temperature for 20 minutes and then turn the oven down to 325°F/165°C/gas mark 3 for the rest of the cooking time. For well-done meat add on another 20 minutes' cooking time. Sprinkle the beef with salt just before serving.

Before making the gravy, remove the beef to a warm place. This might be the turned-off oven, but if you are continuing to use the oven, wrap the beef instead, first in foil and then in a thick towel. This 'resting' relaxes the meat and makes it easier to carve. Pour most of the fat out of the roasting pan. Set it on medium heat on top of the stove. Using a wooden spoon, stir in 2 teaspoonfuls of flour and push it around, gathering up any little crusty bits. When the flour is browned, pour in about ½ pint/290 ml stock or vegetable cooking water. Adding a tablespoonful of red wine or soy sauce will enhance the flavour. Bring to the boil and keep stirring until the gravy is smooth. Taste, and add salt and pepper if necessary. When you carve the meat, add the juices that run from the joint to the gravy.

## YORKSHIRE PUDDING

See the recipe in Chapter One (p.15).

## ROAST PORK

The cheaper cuts of pork, such as belly or hand, roast well. Their higher fat content keeps them moist during cooking. Leg and loin are the more expensive parts of pork sold for roasting. One of the great assets of roast pork is the crackling and it is important that this is scored, i.e. cut into strips before the meat goes in the oven. If this has not been done sufficiently well by the butcher, roast the pork for 30 minutes, then remove from the oven — the skin will have softened and it will be easy to cut. Sprinkling the pork with salt before cooking helps to crisp the skin.

Roast pork at 400°F/200°C/gas mark 6 for 25 minutes per 1 lb/450 g plus an extra 25 minutes. It is the one meat that you do not want rare, or pink, in any part. If you have a glass of white or red wine on hand, pour it into the roasting tin around the meat when you put it into the oven. It will make a nice, clear gravy. Check during cooking to see if the wine has dried up and if so, add a glass of water. To make a thicker gravy, follow the instructions given above for roast beef.

## ROAST LAMB

The joints of lamb most usually sold for roasting are shoulder and leg, the shoulder being cheaper but harder to carve and with less meat on it. The flavourings that suit lamb very well are garlic and rosemary. If you like garlic it is worth peeling a clove and cutting it into small strips, then with a small sharp knife making a slit here and there in the flesh of the lamb and pushing the garlic in. This flavours the meat throughout during cooking.

Brush the joint of lamb with vegetable oil. If you have some rosemary, either dried or fresh, scatter a few strands in the bottom of the roasting pan and some over the meat. Sprinkle salt and pepper on the meat and roast it for 30 to 35 minutes per 1 lb/450 g for leg and 40 minutes per 1 lb/450 g for shoulder, with the oven turned to 350°F/180°C/gas mark 4. Instead of making gravy, which goes less well with lamb than with other roast meats, add a cup of stock and a splash of wine, if you have any around, to the juices in the roasting pan and bubble them together on the top of the stove, scraping all the sediment loose with a wooden spoon. Taste for seasoning and add salt and pepper if necessary.

**Important note:** Carving any joint takes time and there is a risk that the meat will cool, so always have warmed plates ready to serve it on.

### Roast Potatoes

There are two things you must not underestimate about roast potatoes: the time it takes to cook them satisfactorily and the number people will eat. Allow one large potato per person with one or two extra. You can roast potatoes in the tin in which the meat is cooking, or in a separate tin — which has the advantage that you can move them to the top of the oven to brown and crisp. Either way, peel the potatoes and cut them into pieces, halves or quarters, so that they all end up about the same size. If you have plenty of time to cook them — 1 to 1½ hours — you can start them raw, but if you have any less time than this it is better to bring the potatoes to the boil in a large pan of water with a teaspoonful of salt and boil them for 5 minutes first. Drain them into a colander or sieve and when they have cooled a little, rough up the surface of the potatoes with a fork. Put them either into the meat tin or into a separate tin in which you have heated some oil, lard or dripping. Using a spatula or serving spoon, turn them around to make sure they are covered with fat. Roast in a hot oven, turning them from time to time, for an hour or more.

### Vegetables

Whatever vegetables you choose to cook with your meal, do not overcook them. This robs them of vitamins and of flavour. If you are using frozen vegetables, test them to see if they are ready before the time given on the packet. Most people nowadays like vegetables to be crisp rather than soggy. If you are making roast meat and roast potatoes then you might think about not doing an accompanying vegetable but serving a green salad afterwards (see Chapter Seven, p.000). This is a particularly good idea with roast chicken.

### Ideas from Other Chapters

## DESSERTS

### CRUMBLES

One of the best of British ideas for a dessert is a crumble. This crunchy topping can be baked on top of any fruit that is in season. Apple is perhaps the most usual base for crumble, but pears, plums, damsons, apricots and rhubarb are also excellent. Simmer your choice of fruit — in the case of apples and pears, peeled and sliced — on top of the stove with a little wtaer and sugar to taste until the fruit is just tender. Prepare the crumble mixture. All this can be done in advance of the meal.

4 oz / 110 g self-raising flour
3 oz / 85 g demerara sugar
6 oz / 170 g butter
3 tbsp muesli (which provides a nice crunch and usually a selection of nuts and dried fruits)

Mix together the flour and sugar. Cut the butter into small cubes and with your fingertips rub it into the flour and sugar until you have a mixture resembling uneven breadcrumbs. Stir in the muesli. Drain off any excess juice from the stewed fruit and keep it aside. Put the fruit in an ovenproof baking dish. Sprinkle the crumble mixture on top and bake in an oven set at 350°F/180°C/gas mark 4 for about 40 minutes. Try to plan your meal so that you are cooking a crumble while you are also using the oven for a roast. Watch that the top browns but does not burn. Serve the crumble with custard, whipped cream, soured cream or Greek yoghurt with a little of the reserved fruit juice stirred into the creams or yoghurt.

### BUTTERSCOTCH SAUCE

A quick and delicious dessert is a good brand of bought ice-cream with a home-made sauce. The combination of warm sauce and cold ice-cream and the changes in texture which that meeting results in are wonderful.

¼ pint / 150 ml corn syrup or maple syrup
6 oz / 170 g brown sugar
pinch of salt
1 oz / 30 g butter
5 tbsp double cream or evaporated milk

Heat the syrup, sugar, salt and butter in a heavy-bottomed saucepan over a very gentle heat until the sugar is dissolved to the point where there is no sight or sound of the crunch of it. Bring the mixture to the boil and cook quickly for 2 minutes. Remove from the heat and leave to cool a little. Stir in the cream or evaporated milk gradually. If you have difficulty in mixing it, stir it over a low heat. Serve warm.

Note: If you make this ahead of time or if you have some left over and want to heat it up, put it in a jam jar (without the lid), put the jar into simmering water and simmer until the sauce is heated through. This should stop the sugar crystallizing.

**Ideas from Other Chapters**
Clafoutis — p.19
Chocolate Mousse — p.54
Fruit Kebabs — p.73
Baked Alaska — p.74
Instant Raspberry Sorbet — p.75

CHAPTER NINE

# FOOD AS PRESENTS AND FOR PARTIES

PEPPERMINT CREAMS · CHOCOLATE CREAMS

ROMANCING THE (DATE) STONE · FLAPJACKS

VANILLA FUDGE · CHOCOLATE FUDGE

BRAMBLE JELLY · DELICIOUS BISCUITS

BROWNIES · TANDOORI CHICKEN DRUMSTICKS

SPARE RIBS · STUFFED PITTA BREAD

CIDER PUNCH

Every meal or dish or snack that you cook and give to others is, in a sense, a present, but there are some items that are particularly suited to being wrapped up prettily and handed out at Christmas, birthdays or when you go to visit. Making the packaging attractive is part of the pleasure. Cardboard boxes can be covered with wrapping paper and lined with paper doilies. Cellophane can be tied round toffee apples or handfuls of fudge, and circles of fabric can be cut out and fastened on to the top of jam jars with an elastic band. A glass jar with a glass stopper adds a present to the present. Make sure the contents of any container are well protected, using greaseproof or kitchen paper, as a parcel of crumbs is a disappointing gift. Everything in this chapter is sweet, and the first two items are uncooked, making them ideal for young cooks working on their own.

## PEPPERMINT CREAMS

1 egg-white
8–10 oz/225–275 g icing sugar
peppermint essence — the amount will depend on how much peppermint flavour you want (see recipe)
4 oz/110 g dark chocolate (if you want to dip the creams)

Put the egg-white in a bowl and beat with a fork until it breaks up into a foam. Sift 8 oz/225 g of the icing sugar into another bowl and stir in the egg-white. You are going to roll out the paste like pastry, so decide if you need more sugar to make it stiffer. The size of the egg-white makes a difference. Add a few drops — about half a teaspoonful — of the peppermint essence and stir some more. Taste and see if you want more

peppermint. Using your hands, knead the mixture, rather as you would dough, until it is smooth. Dust a work surface with icing sugar and rub some on your rolling-pin. Roll out the mixture to a thickness of about ¼ in/0.5 cm. Use a small biscuit-cutter to cut out rounds. Cover a wire cooling-rack with greaseproof paper and put the creams on it to dry. Leave for an hour or so.

### Chocolate Creams

Break up the chocolate and put it into a china bowl that will sit in a saucepan. Bring water to the boil in the saucepan and, when it has boiled, remove it from the heat and sit the bowl of chocolate over it. When the chocolate has melted, stir it until it is smooth and glossy and then remove it from the saucepan of hot water and let it cool a little. Dip half of each peppermint cream into the chocolate. Replace them on the greaseproof paper and leave them to set. Do not store these creams in the fridge. Put them in an airtight tin with layers of greaseproof paper or foil between them.

## ROMANCING THE (DATE) STONE

half a packet (usually sold as 8 oz/225 g) of marzipan
about 20 dates
caster sugar (optional)

Make a slit in the top of each date and carefully remove the stones. Roll the marzipan into a snake about the width of a stone and pinch off lengths the length of a date. Roll each of these pieces into an oval with pointed ends and push them into the spaces left by the stones. Press the date round the marzipan filling and if you want to give the dates a frosted finish, roll them in caster sugar. Left-over marzipan can be used for cakes or coloured with food colouring and shaped into 'fruits'. Wrapped in clingfilm, marzipan will keep for a couple of months in the refrigerator.

## FLAPJACKS

Although these chewy biscuits do require some cooking, they are so easy they almost seem instant.

1 tbsp flour, for preparing the tin
8 oz/225 g dark brown sugar
8 oz/225 g butter
1 tbsp golden syrup
12 oz/340 g rolled oats

Makes about 20 small flapjacks

Turn on the oven to 350°F/180°C/gas mark 4.

With a little butter on a piece of kitchen paper, grease a tin 8 in x 10 in/20 cm x 25 cm, and then shake a spoonful of flour around the inside and pour off the excess. Melt the butter and sugar in a large saucepan over a low heat. Add the golden syrup and stir until that has melted. Stir in the rolled oats. Press the mixture into the prepared tin and cook in the oven for 30 minutes. Remove the tin from the oven, using thick oven gloves, and divide the mixture into squares while it is still warm.

## VANILLA FUDGE

1 lb/450 g granulated sugar
4 oz/110 g butter
¼ pint/150 ml milk
¼ pint/150 ml condensed milk
3 drops vanilla essence

If you have no sugar thermometer, fill a cup with cold water and sit it near the stove. With a little oil or butter, grease a tin about 6 in x 8 in/15 cm x 20 cm and line it with greaseproof paper. The oiliness of the tin will make the paper stick to the base and sides. Place all the ingredients in a heavy-bottomed saucepan and put on a low heat. Stir until the sugar has completely dissolved. When you have a smooth mixture with no sight or sound of the crunch of sugar, bring it to the boil and boil until the mixture starts to come away from the side of the pan and it has reached the 'soft ball' stage. This is 250°F/120°C on a sugar thermometer and you can test the temperature by dripping a few drops of the mixture into the cup of cold water. They should immediately form a soft ball that holds together. When it is at the right temperature, take the pan of fudge off the heat and beat it with a wooden spoon for a few minutes. As it cools, the mixture starts to thicken. Pour into the prepared tin and leave to set. When it is firm, cut into squares with a knife.

## CHOCOLATE FUDGE

1 x 14 oz/400 g tin of condensed milk
12 oz/340 g granulated sugar
5 oz/140 g butter
1 generous tbsp cocoa powder (*not* drinking chocolate)
3 drops vanilla essence

Prepare a tin as described in the Vanilla Fudge recipe above. Place all the ingredients in a heavy-bottomed saucepan and heat over a low heat until the sugar has dissolved and there is no feeling of grittiness. Bring to the boil and stir with a wooden spoon until the mixture thickens. Take the pan from the heat and beat hard for a minute. Pour into the prepared tin. When the fudge sets, cut into squares with a knife.

Note: Vanilla Fudge and Chocolate Fudge mixed together make a very seductive present.

## BRAMBLE JELLY

Blackberries are one of the most plentiful and best of the 'free' foods. If you have the opportunity to pick a quantity you can make this jelly, which is lovely balanced on bread and butter and unbeatable with Panscones (see Chapter One, p.19) and cream. No one can fail to be pleased with this hedgerow present.

as many blackberries as you can collect
granulated sugar or preserving sugar — 1 lb/ 450 g for every 1 pint/570 ml of blackberry juice
juice of 1 or 2 lemons, depending on the quantity of fruit (allow 1 lemon per 2 lb/1 kg of fruit)

Wash the blackberries quickly and then drain them. Put them in a heavy-bottomed saucepan and add enough water barely to come level with the top layer. Cook the fruit slowly, mashing it with a wooden spoon until soft and broken up — about 30 minutes. Either fix up a large sieve over a bowl and line the sieve with a clean tea-towel wrung out in very hot water, or, if you have a jelly-bag in the house, hang this over a bowl. Leave the blackberry mixture to drain for several hours or overnight in order that the last drip drips through. Measure the juice, pour it into a large pan and add the correct amount of sugar. Add in the lemon juice. Heat up the mixture slowly and let the sugar dissolve. When it has completely dissolved, bring to a fast boil and boil for 10 minutes. Take the pan off the heat and pour a little of the juice on to a saucer. Put the saucer into the refrigerator or freezer for a minute or two. Take it out and push the blackberry liquid with your forefinger. If the surface wrinkles, the jelly will set. If it doesn't, boil the blackberry juice for a further 5 minutes and test again. When it is ready, ladle it into jam jars that you have washed out in very hot water. Cover when cool, using either the original jam-jar lids or the paper discs you can buy.

Bramble Jelly

## DELICIOUS BISCUITS

This recipe could hardly be simpler, but it makes a good biscuit that takes well to being iced with plain icing or dipped into chocolate or, with the addition of 1 teaspoonful of ground ginger into the mixture, fashioned into gingerbread men, with currants for eyes and noses and chips of glacé cherries for mouths.

Makes about 24 biscuits

4 oz/110 g butter
4 oz/110 g caster sugar
8 oz/225 g plain flour
1 egg (size 3 or 4)

Let the butter sit at room temperature until it is soft. Put the butter and sugar into a large mixing bowl and beat together with a wooden spoon. Beat the egg in a small bowl. Add it to the butter and sugar mixture and beat it in. Sift in the flour and stir that in and, if necessary, use your fingers to pinch the mixture together to a stiff dough. The dough will be easier to handle if you now let it sit for an hour in the refrigerator, but you can continue straight away.

Turn on the oven to 375°F/190°C/gas mark 5.

Rub a smear of butter or oil on to a baking sheet and dust it with plain flour.

Roll out the dough on a lightly floured work surface until it is about ¼ in/0.5 cm thick. Cut into shapes either with biscuit-cutters or with a sharp knife. If you are making gingerbread men, now is the moment to put on their faces. Place the biscuits on the prepared baking sheet and cook them in the top half of the oven for 10 minutes. Using oven gloves, take out the tin, remove the biscuits with a spatula and let them cool on a wire rack.

You can dip the biscuits into melted chocolate, following the instructions in the Peppermint Creams recipe, or mix 2 oz/55 g icing sugar with just enough lemon juice (about a teaspoonful) to make an icing and spoon that on.

## BROWNIES

Makes about 16 brownies

4 oz/110 g butter
4 oz/110 g plain chocolate
8 oz/225 g caster sugar
2 eggs
4 oz/110 g plain flour
½ tsp baking powder
pinch of salt
2 oz/55 g chopped walnuts (optional)
a few drops of vanilla essence

Turn on the oven to 325°F/170°C/gas mark 3.

Grease a square cake tin about 8 in x 10 in/ 20 cm x 25 cm with a little butter. In a large saucepan set over a very low heat, melt the butter and the chocolate which you have broken into pieces. Remove from the stove and stir well with a wooden spoon. Stir in the sugar. Add the eggs and the vanilla essence (drip it in off the end of a skewer). Beat well with the wooden spoon. Sift in the flour and salt, add the nuts if you are using them and stir until well mixed. Spread the mixture in the cake tin. Put in the oven and cook for 30 to 35 minutes. Using stout oven gloves, remove the pan and leave the mixture to cool. It will sink, but this is quite right — the point about brownies is that they have a sticky inside and a crusty top which is due to using twice the amount of sugar as of flour. Before the cake is quite cold, cut it into squares with an oiled knife. When cold, wrap each square in Cellophane or greaseproof paper and store in a tin or pack up for friends.

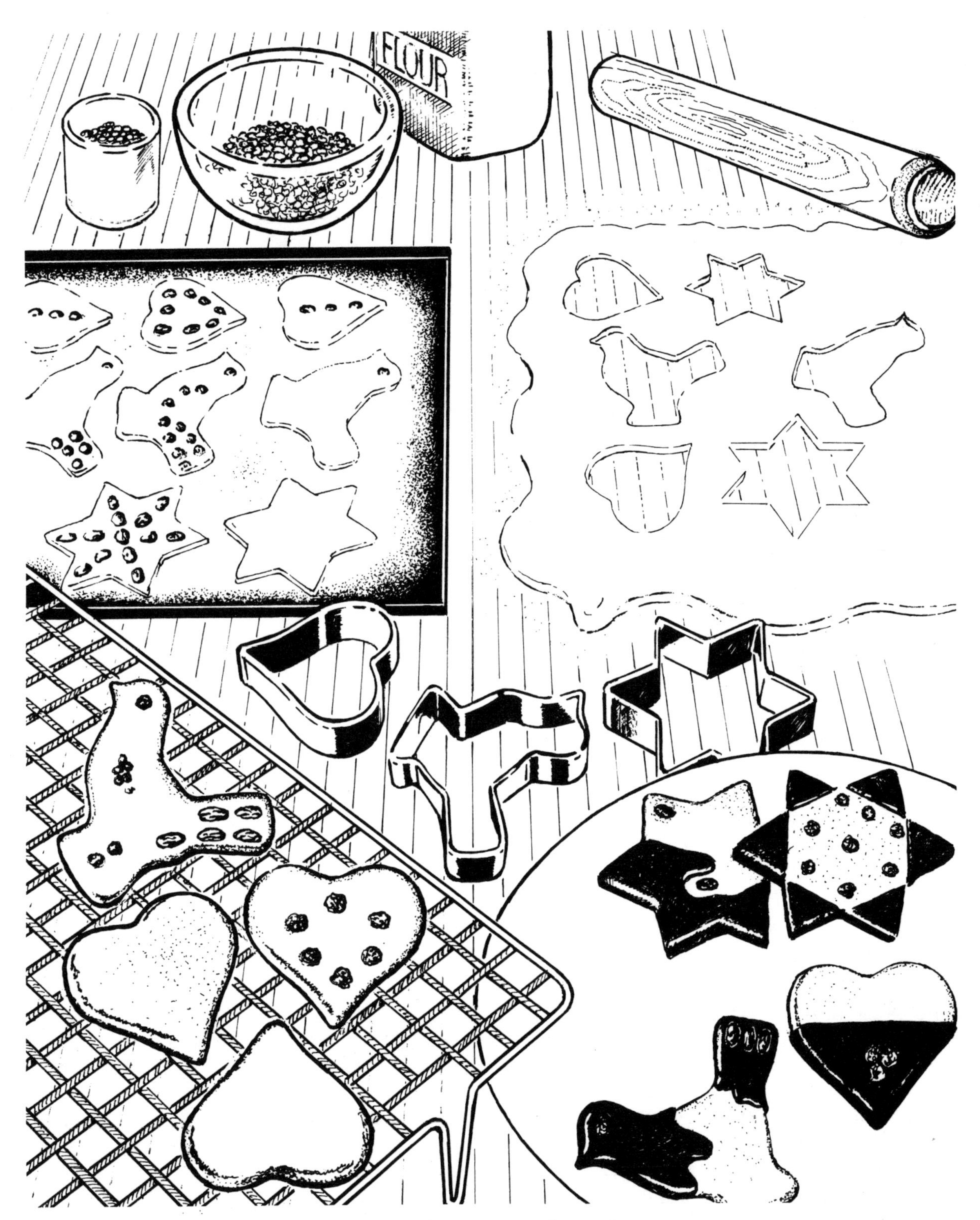


Delicious Biscuits

## Parties

Having gained confidence about food preparation and cooking, you might want to entertain, give a party. Many of the recipes in the previous chapters can be adapted to partying; a list of the appropriate ones is given at the end of this section.

One of the puzzles with regard to feeding numbers of people is how much food to prepare. It seems mingy and inhospitable not to make enough and so to run out, but on the other hand you do not want to end up with more left-overs than you can cope with. The recipes in this chapter are for quantities to feed 12, and ideas from other chapters can be multiplied according to the numbers they were originally designed to feed. Keep in mind the odd fact that the more people you feed, the less they eat per head.

Hand-held food, food you can pick up and wander around with — for example chicken drumsticks, slices of pizza and quiche, small vol-au-vents, crudités, spare ribs and stuffed pitta bread — tends to get eaten in greater quantities and disappear faster than dishes you spoon on to a plate — such as moussaka, lasagne, chilli con carne and pasta.

Food for a party should be easy to eat — requiring a plate and a fork at the most. When you lay the table for a party, do it in a logical fashion, starting at one end with the piles of plates, moving on to the main dishes, the salads, then breads (garlic bread is a welcome guest at any party) and cheese if you are serving it, and finishing with the cutlery and a large supply of paper napkins. If you have enough space, put drinks and glasses on a separate table.

Something sweet to finish with might be a cake, if it is a birthday party, or items such as brandysnaps, brownies and meringues — all of which your guests can eat without making too much mess or even needing another plate. Fruit kebabs (Chapter Six) are an ideal party dessert; refreshing and neat to eat. If you want to focus on the sweet side of things, letting guests put together their own ice-cream sundaes is an idea. Lay out scoops of various flavours of ice-cream, chopped fruit, chocolate and butterscotch sauces, chopped nuts, whipped cream and so on. The drawback to this idea is that people can get more interested in the creating than in the consuming.

### TANDOORI CHICKEN DRUMSTICKS

You could grind your own spices to make this, but the tandoori mixture sold ready-prepared works well and gives you the cheerful red colour associated with this method of preparing chicken. Bear in mind that you must start this recipe the day before the party.

Serves 12

30 chicken drumsticks
juice of two small lemons
2 tsp salt

*For the marinade:*
3 dsp from a 4 oz/113 g tin of tandoori mixture
1 carton plain yoghurt
3 tbsp wine vinegar
1 tbsp lemon juice
2 tbsp vegetable oil

Using small sharp knife, make a few short slits in each chicken leg. This will help the marinade to sink in. If you wish you can skin the chicken legs, but some people (including the author of this book) think that the skin is almost the best part of chicken. Put the drumsticks in a large bowl or two bowls. Pour the lemon juice over and sprinkle with the salt and, with your fingers, rub the lemon and salt into the chicken. Mix together the ingredients for the marinade. Pour it on to the chicken and turn the pieces in it until they are well coated, pushing some of the mixture into the slits. Cover and leave in a cool place or in the refrigerator overnight.

Turn on the oven to 475°F/240°C/gas mark 8.

Take the chicken from the marinade, letting the excess mixture drip back into the bowl. Lay the drumsticks in a single layer in one or two roasting pans. Cook for 25 to 30 minutes, turning the drumsticks once and switching the roasting tins around if you are using two, one above the other. Serve hot, warm or cold with lemon wedges and either warm pitta bread or nan bread. Green salad goes well.

## SPARE RIBS

Practically everyone loves spare ribs and you can serve them warm or cool as well as hot. To cook spare ribs in quantity it is easier if you buy them in racks rather than cut up singly. If necessary, roast them in batches and slice the ribs apart before serving. Make sure you ask the butcher for the American cut of spare ribs which are the bones with not much meat attached.

5 lb/2.3 kg spare ribs

*For the cooking suace:*
8 tbsp tomato ketchup
3 tbsp clear honey or golden syrup
1 level dsp made mustard
2 tbsp vegetable oil
4 tbsp soy sauce
a few vigorous shakes from the Worcestershire sauce bottle

Turn on the oven to 475°F/240°C/gas mark 8.

Trim any obvious lumps of fat from the racks of ribs. With a small sharp knife, cut down about 1 in/2 cm between the bones. Mix together the ingredients for the sauce. Using a pastry brush, coat both sides of the racks of ribs with some of the sauce. Arrange the ribs in a roasting dish, preferably on a wire rack to keep them from cooking in the sauce. Cook for 20 to 30 minutes on one side. Using stout oven gloves, remove the pans from the oven. Paint the ribs with more of the sauce on the top side, then turn them over and paint the other side. Roast for a further 20 to 30 minutes. If you have time and opportunity it helps to baste the ribs (brush them with the sauce) a few times during the cooking, but take care with the hot pans. Divide the ribs into single bones and keep warm in a low oven until ready to serve.

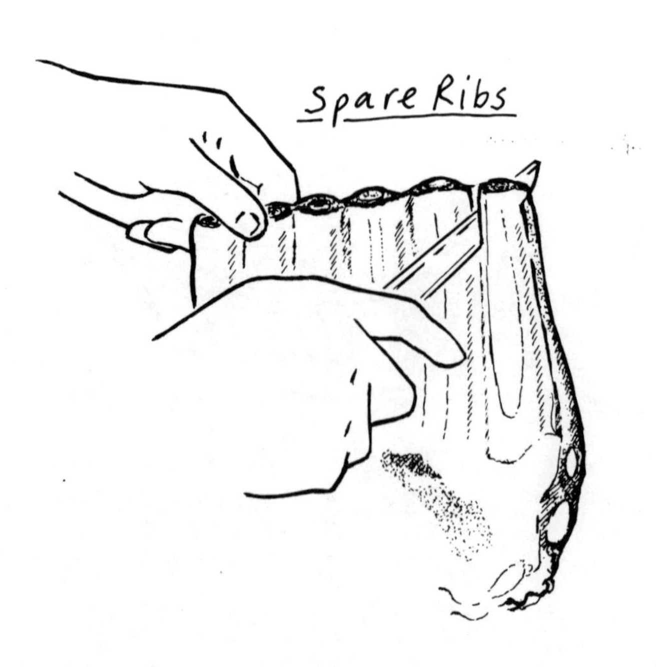

## STUFFED PITTA BREAD

Pitta bread makes wonderful containers for food, and if you offer a selection of fillings you can please most of the people most of the time. There are few things in life more disappointing than unwarmed pitta bread, so make sure that you heat the breads (cut in half across the middle) in a medium oven for about 10 minutes just before the eating starts. If you are cooking for a bonfire party, stuff the pitta halves with fillings that are good hot, such as sausages or minced meat. Wrap them in foil and heat them in the embers of the fire.

**Possible Fillings**

Crisply fried bacon with Guacamole (Chapter Seven)
Prawns in Cocktail Sauce (Chapter Eight)
Grilled sausages or frankfurters with a selection of mustards and pickles and spring onions
Tuna Salad with shredded lettuce (Chapter Seven)
Sautéd minced meat (Chapter Five)
Chinese Scrambled Eggs (Chapter Four)

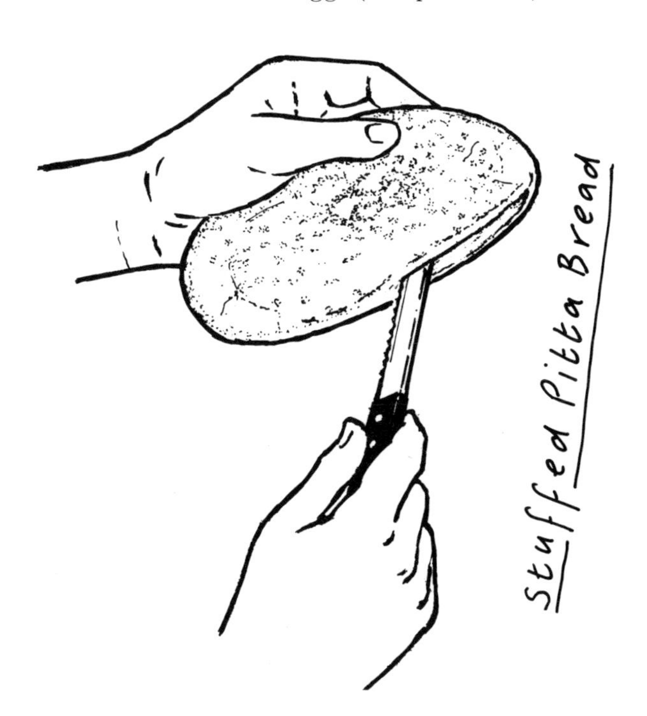


## DRINKS

What you have to drink depends of course on the age of the people at the party and on your own preference. Serve only a small selection, as this saves too many glasses getting used as well as being easier to organize. Some sort of cup or punch is always popular. The one below is very mildly alcoholic and is refreshing.

## CIDER PUNCH

2 pints/1 litre cider
2 pints/1 litre tonic water
2 x 6¼ oz/175 g carton of frozen orange juice
2 oranges, sliced

Chill the cider and tonic water in the refrigerator. Make up the frozen orange juice with cold water to give you 2 pints/1 litre of juice. Mix the juice with the cider and tonic and, just before serving, add the orange slices and some ice cubes.

**Other Recipes in the Book Suitable for Parties**

Vol-au-Vents — p.25
Lasagne — p.27
Quiche Lorraine (Egg and Bacon Tart) — p.52
Chocolate Mousse — p.54
Tuiles d'Amandes (Almond Tiles) — p.57
Shepherd's Pie — p.62
Moussaka — p.63
Chilli con Carne — p.63
Fruit Kebabs — p.73
Brandysnaps — p.75
Crudités with Dips — p.78
Hummus — p.80
Pizza — p.87
Caesar Salad Almost — p.89
Garlic Bread — p.89
Butterscotch Sauce — p.97
Flapjacks — p.102
Brownies — p.104

The following lists indicate which of the recipes in the book are particularly easy, quick or cheap or are 'sweet treat' favourites that you might like to make for a party — or just for fun.

**Easy**



**Quick**



**Cheap**

**Sweet Treats**